CW00850712

THE VILLAGE OF ASTLEY BRIDGE

By Norman Hindley

Dedicated to the memory of the author Norman Hindley who unfortunately passed away before he could finish his book and I was unable to publish it as promised.. This is the fulfilment of that promise

2Copyright @ Alan Rigby

2021

All proceeds from this book will be donated to The Friends of Astley Bridge.

ISBN 978-0-9935795--0-9

In memory of the author Norman Hindley for
his lifetime love of Local History,
Reminiscence and Astley Bridge.

The Village of Astley Bridge.
by
Norman Hindley

All the material contained in this volume is just as Norman
left it in 2020. It has been collated and published by Alan
Rigby in fulfilment of a promise to do so, when it was
completed. This unfortunately was not able to happen so it is
printed in the order Norman left it together with an
addendum of pages numbered 171 to 190 that I feel were to
be the completion of his work. There is a page missing
number 181-182, that was probably to be about the sinking
of Titanic but I feel it would be wrong for me to add my
version, so I leave it to the reader to research as Norman
would have done.

For Ruby and Hilary with thanks
for their permission for me to carry out my
promise to Norman.

ASTLEY BRIDGE

1904

Going back to the 1700s prior to the Eagley and New Eagley mills being built, the area we now call Astley Bridge was a far different place to what it is today. It was beautiful area of hilly green fields, woodland, and sparkling brooks which would be teaming with fish. The Industrial Revolution was in its infancy and the water in these brooks was pure and unpolluted. There were farms dotting the area with little knots of cottages here and there, mainly around Viola Street (Kellys Row), Cottages on Blackburn Road, Skrike Row, Lamb Brow, Old Road, Belmont Road, Greenwood Vale. Moss Lea, Oldhams Cottages, Pemberton Street, Ramsey Street, Springfield Cottages now Whitehill. Horrocks Fold, Eagley Bank, Sharples Park, Birley Street and Bank Top Village which came with the building of New Eagley Mills. Most of the stone properties in these areas are listed buildings.

In those days the main route to Blackburn through Astley Bridge from Bolton was up Lamb Brow, Old Road, Broad O'th Lane, and Bar Lane, turning left into what is now Blackburn Road A666, up to and into Andrew Lane, Hough Lane onto Cox Green, then turning left towards the Unitarian Chapel and on through the hamlet of Dimple. The remains of the old road can be seen today running parallel with, and on the left hand side of the current Blackburn Road just after passing what was the King William Public House, which is now an Italian Restaurant, firstly called Baroccos and now Ciao Baby.

Astley Bridge is a bit of a hybrid as it was created mainly from the Manor of Sharples, a little from the Manor of Longworth, and also Little Bolton.

How it got its name is a bit of a mystery, some say it is a corruption of two words namely ast and ley. In old English, ast meant ash and ley meant clearing, so Astley suggests clearing in a wood of ash trees. An old map of the area does show on the south side of the village woodland of ash and sycamore trees. Interestingly there were houses in the area, Ash Grove, and Ash Bank

Personally I do not think that this is where the name came from as there is evidence of a family named Astley who in 1557 bought a piece of land from the Manor of Sharples. The Manor covered a great area of some 3,999 acres taking in Winter Hill, Whimberry Hill, goes to the west and north, through Smithills, Rivington, and Anglezarke, also Belmont village going down to Little Bolton. The land bought was part of Lower Sharples.

In Higher Sharples there was a big house called Beau Mount, could this be where Belmont got its name?

When people travelled through this land to Blackburn and the north they probably referred to it as Astley's land and with the bridge being the start of their land it took the Astley name, or maybe there was a ford crossing and the Astley family replaced the ford with a bridge.

Astley Bridge people were proud of their village, and their independence, becoming part of Bolton for many if not most of the villagers was not welcome. Even as late as the 1940s people would say "I am going to Bolton." Whereas today people say "I am going to town" However as the older generation passed away and new estates were built in Astley Bridge, the feeling of independence from Bolton has virtually gone.

Astley Bridges population in
      1801 was 873
      1851 was 2,880
      1901 was 7,674
      1951 was 10,113
      1986 was 12,900
      2001 was 13,008 of which 6278 were men, 6730 were
             women. There were 12,298 Whites, 124 Mixed, 499
             Asian, 42 Black, 41 Chinese.

The increase in population was obviously due to the building of more mills in the village. One interesting fact was that it took another 50 years after New Eagley mills were built for another mill to come on stream and the population figures back up this fact. However the decline in the cotton industry, and the closing of mills in the 1950s should have meant a levelling of the population. The reason this did not happen was there was a great increase in house building mainly in the north of Astley Bridge from Crompton Way to Ashworth Lane, including Bank top through to Andrew Lane, and also on the north side of Bar Lane from Blackburn road to Belmont Road. Oldhams Council Estate was also built in the early 1950s. This helped to make Astley Bridge a commuter belt for Bolton and beyond.

ASTLEY BRIDGE BECOMING PART OF BOLTON

In the Directories of the late 1800s and early 1900s kept in the council's archives, we are told in the Past and Present section. "The Queens diamond Jubilee year (1898) synchronises with the greatest and most significant event in the history of the town during Her Majesty's reign. On numerous occasions during the past thirty years attempts have been made to obtain an extension of the Municipal boundaries of the Borough. Again and again facts bearing on the question were compiled, and evidence accumulated. Applications have been made to Parliament with this object in view, and have been refused. Commissioners have held official enquiries in the town, but results have been almost nil. The extensions secured after Herculean efforts were comparatively insignificant. Bolton continued with a smaller acreage than, and consequently was one of the most crowded of all the great towns of the Kingdom.
But all this has changed as stated at the time as if by an enchanter's wand, or the imposition of some miraculous agency. It is only an act of bare justice to say that the altered conditions of the problem, ending in a happy solution, were largely the handiwork of Sir Benjamin Dobson." Then the text continues with further points such as. "The vast addition of territory and of population to the Borough is rendering necessary various important undertakings some of which have already become urgent. One of the most pressing of these is the need of a superior tram service. The text finally ends with, "Improved inter-communication will be one of the surest agencies for further development and the full utilisation of the increased resources of a Greater Bolton."

SIR BENJAMIN ALBERT DOBSON

Mayor of Bolton 1894-8
Born Douglas Isle of Man 27th October 1847
Died Doffcockers Bolton 4th March 1898
Buried at St. Peter's Halliwell
Industrialist
Lt Colonel 27th Lancashire Rifle Volunteers
Alderman for North Ward
Made a Magistrate in 1880
Cut the first sod in Heaton Cemetery 11th April 1878
Opened Chadwick Museum 12th June 1884
Knighted 21st July 1897.
His wife Coralie first Mayoress to wear the chain and badge 9th
May 1895
Coralie died 1904
He was a Governor of Bolton School
He presented Crompton's original mule to Bolton Museum
He patented 22 inventions
In 1890 as a celebration of the companies centenary over 3.500
employees were treated to a trip to the seaside, they filled 6
trains.

 D A Farnie tells us that Sir Benjamin was a direct descendant of the Dobson's of Westmoreland, having had land near Patterdale from the 15th Century. In 1864 he was a mechanical engineer on the Belfast and Northern Counties Railway. In 1869 he came to work in Bolton at Dobson's which was managed by his uncle. The company was founded by Isaac Dobson a cabinet maker in 1790, and Peter Rothwell a timber merchant. The business was passed to a nephew of Isaac's namely Benjamin then to his son also called Benjamin who in 1851 took into partnership Edward Barlow. On the death of Edward Barlow in 1868, the company still kept the title Dobson and Barlow's. Being the great grandson of Isaac Dobson's brother Sir Benjamin became the fourth generation of the family in the business. He died at the age of 51 and he had a military funeral on 7th March 1898 which was attended by 20,000 people, mourners came in 300 carriages together with 33 clergymen. His estate was £240,134/9/10 Dobson and Barlow's were one of the oldest engineering works in the world and by 1860 they employed over 1,500 people.

In 1906 they opened another manufacturing base at Bradley Fold. They manufactured all kinds of machinery for the cotton mills, and by 1914 their workforce numbered 5,000.

In World War 1 they suspended making textile machinery and concentrated on the production on various kinds of armaments for the war effort such as, hand grenades, shells, mines, searchlights and field kitchens.

After the war ended they reverted back to manufacturing textile machinery as a number of European countries needed to refurbish their cotton mills which had been destroyed or damaged during the war. In the early thirties Dobson and Barlow's transferred all their production to their Bradley Fold works and many people, in fact, around 1,000 lost their jobs.

In the 2nd World War the company produced bomber wings.

After various mergers with other companies, and with competition from the Far East growing, and also the Lancashire cotton industry in decline, with mills closing virtually daily. The company shrunk and by 1979 Dobson and Barlow's workforce was less than 200.

Dobson and Barlow's were renowned for having the tallest chimney in England. Octagonal in shape, it was 367 feet 6 inches in height, 42 feet 6 inches in diameter at the base, and 24 feet in diameter at the top. Just short of one million bricks were used in its construction together with about 120 ton of stone. It is said that it took only 16 weeks to build. It was known as "Little John" 4,000 people made the journey by hoist to the top on completion. Whilst it is known affectionately by Boltonians as Dobson and Barlow's chimney, it was built for Blinkhorn's Chemical Works and was completed in 1834. There had been many complaints from the local residents about the awful smells coming from the works chimneys, so it was decided to build a very tall chimney to disperse the problem noxious fumes, unfortunately the tall chimney did not quite resolve the problem and It was finally demolished in 1967 having been reduced in size a number of times earlier in its life.

The Manchester Guardian of 23rd January 1847 reports that John and James Dodd who were competitors of Blinkhorns in the chemical industry, decided to build a chimney larger than Blinkhorns. This reached a height of 420 feet, unfortunately the foundations started to give way, the stack started to lean, then the whole structure collapsed.

Whilst Blinkhorns chimney was the largest chimney in England when it was completed, it was dwarfed by "Tenants Stalk" in Glasgow, a chimney reaching a height of 455 feet. It belonged to Tenant's Chemical Works and was the highest chimney in the world. It was taken down in the 1920s which was a very dangerous operation and cost the lives of four workmen.

HOMES OF SIR BENJAMIN DOBSON

Merehall Park 1908

Sir Benjamin Dobson nephew of Isaac Dobson built Mere Hall around 1836; it became a public park in 1890 after being bought by J.P.Thommason a benefactor of Bolton.

DOFFCOCKERS

The home of Dobson and Barlow magnate and Mayor of Bolton, Sir Benjamin Alfred Dobson and his wife, Lady Coralie

Dobson. The Doffcockers stood in its own grounds off Chorley Old Road, was demolished after the death of Lady Dobson and the estate used for housing development.

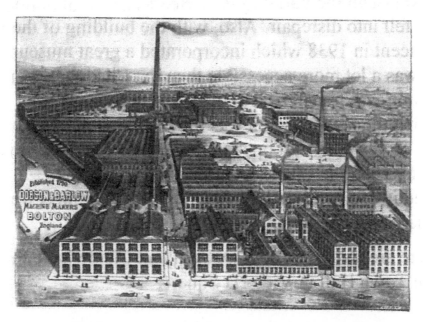

Dobson and Barlow's Waterloo Street

In 1876, Samuel Taylor Chadwick, a local medical doctor of some wealth, died. Chadwick had already gifted the Chadwick Orphanage to the town, and had done many other good works related to children's health and welfare.

Chadwick left a bequest of £5000 to the Bolton Corporation for the 'building, furnishing and maintenance of a Museum of Natural History in the Bolton Park' (later renamed Queen's Park). The bequest came with the conditions that the museum had to be free entry and the museum building had to be erected in 4 years, or the fund would be lost. The building began in 1878. The sub-committee concerned with overseeing the building of the museum was chaired by Councillor B. A. Dobson from the family of cotton machine manufacturers that had founded the firm Dobson and Barlow. Dobson provided great deal of support to the fledgling museum donating and facilitating donations to the collections. The Chadwick Natural History Museum was opened by Dobson on the 12th June 1884.

10

The museum had a great Egyptian Collection, in fact one of the best in the country after the British Museum, thanks to Annie Barlow, a well known local Egyptologist who sadly past away in 1946. Although the building was used as a school during the last war it fell into disrepair. Also, with the building of the Le Mans Crescent in 1938 which incorporated a great museum area, and was a lot more accessible than the Chadwick, part of the collection was transferred to the Le Mans. The B.E.N reported that the new museum was the most modern in the country. The new museum opened to the public 20th October 1947 and by 1955 the Chadwick had closed, and was demolished in 1957. It is said that some of the artefacts were left in the cellars of the building.

Today there are statues of both Dobson and Chadwick either side of the Town Hall in Victoria Square.

CHADWICK MUSEUM

ASTLEY BRIDGE FINALLY JOINS BOLTON

In 1897 the County Borough extension of Bolton Act came about. At that time town was bursting at the seams. Bolton needed more space and with the Extension Act it took other areas under its wing.

In 1897 the County Borough of extension of Bolton came about and up to this time the Bolton union was made up of :- Great and Little Bolton, Halliwell , Haulgh, and Rumworth. Areas to be added were Astley Bridge, Breightmet, Darcy Lever, Deane, Great Lever, Heaton, Lostock, Middle Hulton, Over Hulton, Smithills, and Tonge. So overnight Bolton quadrupled its size. There were little pockets of Little Bolton within the boundaries of Astley Bridge around Sharples Park, and just below Dunscar. How this came about is a mystery.

Astley Bridge people were very proud of their village and were not happy at being taken over by big brother Bolton, they were more than reluctant to join the "Bolton Club" when Bolton wanted to extend its boundaries, and in the early days of negotiations the villagers of Astley Bridge were reluctant to give up all their freedoms and responsibilities and were not interested in being swallowed up by Bolton.

However the Astley Bridge people did get some concessions to help them agree to join the town of Bolton. These sweeteners help to heal the wounds of a very proud village.

1 The rates levied would be 1/6 in the pound for the first 15 years. Thereafter for 35 years Astley Bridge would pay 3d in the pound less than the rest of Bolton.

2 Astley Bridge would have 3 Councillors and an Alderman

3 Astley Bridge would have its own Maintenance Yard for Street lighting Roads, and Scavenging, the yard was behind the

Public Offices on Heywood Street which became Cavendish Street and now is Moss Bank Way. The Offices were opened in 1898 at a cost of £1,930. However Bolton would be responsible for the maintenance of Blackburn Road, Belmont Road and Scout Road.

4 Bolton Corporation would take over Astley Bridge Tram System. Incidentally, the official inauguration of the Bolton tramways system was a journey from Bolton Town Hall to Moses Gate and it was a blue Astley Bridge tram the made the journey. Horse trams first started to operate to Moses Gate, Halliwell and Dunscar on1st September 1880.
Although the original tram tracks were jointly owned by Bolton, Astley Bridge, and Farnworth they were leased to Holden's who ran the system until the end of 1899 when Bolton took over the system from Holden's which included 48 tramcars and 350 horses. On the 2nd January 1900 an electrified system started to various places including Astley Bridge.

5 Bolton agreed to take over Astley Bridge Sewage system.

The cost of Astley Bridge's Tramlines was from the Bolton boundary, i.e Astley Bridge to Cheetham Arms 2585 yards £7,252/3/4 and from Cheetham Arms to Dunscar Bridge 651 yards £1,826/7/5 in total 3236 yards and costing £9078/10/9 roughly £4900 per mile. The village had its own trams which were coloured blue. In fact the horse tram taking the Mayor and Civil Dignitaries on official duty celebrating the building of the new tram system was an Astley Bridge tram. The journey was from the Town Hall to Moses gate.

ASTLEY BRIDGE BOUNDARY

On the opening of the Astley Bridge library in 1910 the Chief Librarian of Bolton, a Mr Archibald Sprake commissioned a map to be made of the village. As Mr Sprake was a stickler for things to be accurate I am sure that the map represented the boundaries to the letter. This map was about six feet square and was hung in the foyer of the Astley Bridge Library. It is now in the Archives in Bolton Civic Centre.

The majority of the village boundary is marked mainly by the brooks Astley, Ravenden, North, and Eagley.

Astley Bridge southern boundary starts at the bridge itself, going west where Astley Brook goes under the buildings on the west of Blackburn Road where originally Knowles garage was, then the site was taken over for Mayoh's Motor body builders, followed by B & Q. The building was then redeveloped as a Snooker Hall. Suddenly after play on Tuesday 20th November 2012, Riley's Snooker Hall closed down apparently without any prior warning. Next to the hall is Viola Street, originally named Kellys Row but the name was changed as were many other streets in the village when Astley Bridge came into Bolton's boundaries under the extension act of 1898.

Street Names were changed due to some names being duplicated in the rest of the Bolton area.

Astley Lane became Waverley Road
Barton Street---Maxwell Street
Church Street---Birley Street
George Street---Drummond Street
Grant Street-----Cameron Street
Heywood Street-Cavendish Street
Howarth Street- Warwick Street

14

Kelly Row—Viola Street
Lower Holland Street-- Palm Street
Rothwell Street --- Ramsey street
Rowland Street—Talbot Street
School Street—Newnham Street
Viola Street –Primula Street   → TAYLOR STREET LLOYD STREET
West Street---Mackenzie Street

Around the same time the houses and shops on Blackburn Road were renumbered by adding 400, so number1 became 401 and so on
As I have already stated Bolton Corporation threw in some sweeteners. Another was that the village could have a committee of three to oversee much of the maintenance of the roads, lighting etc. The exception to this was that Bolton would look after Blackburn Road, Belmont Road, and Scout Road. I feel sure that the three man committee were pleased with this arrangement as these were the major roads through the village and would carry the highest cost to maintain. The village had its own maintenance yard at the back of the library.
As I have said before Bolton promised some inducements, that the borough rate was lower in the village for a further fifty years etc. So Astley Bridge did not join Bolton completely until 1948 when the village came into line with the rest of the town completely. Consequently the three man committee was disbanded and everything was handed over to Bolton Council.

The boundary continues from Blackburn Road following Astley Brook from the bridge going to the west.
On both sides of the brook we pass mixture of buildings and workshops, and somewhere about here Mr James Kenyon set up his "Snowfecta" soap powder factory. The slogan for the powder was "Snowfecta's" knack saves mothers back".
The Astley brook runs behind Greenhalgh and Shaw's cotton mill, then into Sharples Vale, passing on its right James

Brimelow Vale Cotton Mill, which became Maxilin Mint Company.

SHARPLES MILL

The brook passes under a road bridge. The road joins Halliwell Road with Blackburn Road, through Raglan Street, past the Weavers Arms known locally as the Mop, Astley Lane, Waverley Road onto Blackburn Road. Sharples Vale cottages stood on the right of the brook but have long since gone.
Its journey takes it to Hill Mill, Britannia Mill which has had a number of trades finally becoming Henry Crossley Packing's, alas now gone and today we find a new private development Smithills Glade Estate. A bridge crosses the stream at this point carrying a narrow cobbled road from Thorns Road. On the Astley Bridge side the brook passes an area where" Eden's Orphanage" and "The Thorns" used to stand, travelling on; we come to a bridge carrying Moss Bank Way This bridge was built in the 1930s as part of a ring road around Bolton.
Under the bridge and running about some hundred yards or so we come to a meeting of two brooks, Dean Brook coming from Barrow Bridge and Ravenden Brook coming from Scout Road. Together they make Astley Brook.
The boundary at this point turns north following Ravenden Brook. Over to the right is Moss Lea Allotments and Bluebell Wood.

16

Further along we come to a road and on the left is Smithills Hall and the Coaching House whilst to the right is Smithills Farm formerly Harricroft Farm. The main building is a listed building and some years ago whilst rebuilding part of the property was blown down in a gale. Across the farm lane are two very old cottages which are also listed. As we follow the stream through Ravenden Wood we come to a clearing in Mutton Clough an ideal place to rest on a long hike and enjoy a bite to eat. The boundary then makes its way to Scout Road passing on the left Bryan Hey Farm where nearby was an old coal pit, whilst this pit isn't in Astley Bridge there are others that are, for instance one in Sweetloves Lane, then another just off Belmont Road very near to the waterworks. There is cobbled path leading from behind Beech Cottage near Barrow Bridge chimney, up to Limefield Road where a tramtrack started on its way over the moorland to Belmont Road. This was to collect coal not only from this pit but also from others on the moor and Astley Bridge.

Across Scout Road the boundary takes in about 4/5ths of Bryan Hey reservoir,

BRYAN HEY   RESERVOIR

Continuing up Smithills Moor just to the left of Lomax Wives Farm, it veers right over Horrocks Moor to North Brook and North Cottage where it turns right again down to Scout Road about 200 yards or so from Belmont Road crossing the Scout it runs nearly parallel with Belmont Road meeting Belmont Road some 3 to 400 yards from the Scout. This area of moorland was a great place to go whimberry picking. In fact it is called Whimberry Hill.

The boundary takes a sharp left turn to Gale Farm, then sharp left again towards the bridge which crosses Longworth brook which flows from Belmont, through the very beautiful Longworth Clough, a favourite place for walkers and for paddling in the brook. I recall before the 2nd world war walking through the Clough in spring and seeing hundreds of wild daffodils, unfortunately they seem to have gone.

At the bridge Longworth brook becomes Eagley Brook. We turn right with the brook and on the right was a row of red brick terraced cottages. There were about ten cottages and I remember as a lad there were two shops in the row, one of which was a good place to get ice cream. The field between the cottages and the brook was a nice place to picnic. The cottages have long since gone and there is no or very little trace that they were ever there.

On the left of the brook facing what was Longworth cottages is Egerton mills. Whilst not being in Astley Bridge they are worth a mention. They were built in 1826 by a Swiss company and Italian money. In 1829 they were taken over by a consortium including Henry and Edmund Ashworth who built New Eagley Mills. They were philanthropists and wanted a better life for their employees. They built model villages at Egerton and also Bank Top.

Egerton Mill was famous for its famous landmark a 62 feet waterwheel.

We move on down to Dunscar Bridge, passing Dunscar Golf Club on our right. The boundary makes its way towards Eagley.

On its left is an industrial estate followed by a sports field and
Eagley Cricket Club. As we reach Eagley Mills which were
built in1796 we come the village of Eagley.

WHILST THE VAN AND THE TWO BUILDINS IN THE FOREGROUND ARE IN
ASTLEY BRIDGE THE REST OF THE BUILDINGS ARE IN EAGLEY

The mills are now mainly apartment blocks. Eagley Brook then
makes its way towards Birtenshaw passing a sewage works and
over a weir. After about three hundred yards it goes under the
narrow Birtenshaw foot bridge.
Not very far from the footbridge, in a field on the Astley Bridge
side of the brook was quite a famous grave. It was the grave of
what must have been a much loved horse called Paddy. It had a
metal headstone and had kerbstones around. Sadly I believe
there is no trace of the grave any more.
A little further along the boundary comes to Ashworth Bottoms
where the New Eagley Mills stood. They were built in 1802 by
Henry and Edmund Ashworth. There is now vey little left of the
mills just a stump of the mill chimney and some derelict walls.

The Ashworth family lived in a mansion called The Oaks which was on the Tonge Moor side of the brook. There was a bridge a cross the river close to the mill. The brook does dog leg to the right where there was a sewage works now defunct, then an arc to the right through Doctors Clough, finishing up just short of Hall i'th wood. Just at this point below Hall I'th Wood was a row of cottages called Pleasant View. The cottages were occupied well after the last war. They were demolished and now there is now no trace of them, Nature has taken over and reclaimed the land, and all that there is left is the old cobbled road which fronted them. Eagley brook makes its way westwards passing Yew Tree Farm on its right, where before the last war was a little café in the middle of a field where people could enjoy some refreshment when out walking.

Again the brook loops to the right going around what originally was Hall I'th Wood Paper Mill. When it closed down as a paper mill the building has been used by various industries over the years. From here the brook makes its way under the bridge on Crompton Way. (Crompton Way was built and opened in 1928) then after a couple of hundred yards it turns right where it joins up with Astley Brook then the two brooks become the River Tonge. Just before the two brooks meet, there was a farm and just beyond this farm was a lodge which belonged to Eden & Thwaites bleachworks.

EDEN AND THWAITES 1927

The entrance to the bleachworks was at the bottom of Tippings Road through an archway.

During the last war the navy used the building as a rum store. You could smell the rum when you were quite a way off the building.

The bleachworks were demolished some years ago and the land has been developed mainly as a leisure time area. There is a multi-screen cinema, a health club, various restaurants, and new apartment buildings.

Before the area was redeveloped Back o'th Bank Power Station was situated further down Tippings Road I remember as lads we used to bathe in the river opposite the power station as surplus hot water was run off into the river, making it nice and warm. Sometime after the war a cooling tower was built on hill on the other side of the river Tonge. Between the tower and the Bolton to Blackburn railway line, was a big sports field with about a dozen football pitches and a changing hut.

Alongside the field were quite a number of allotments. The Sports field has also been redeveloped, with Beloit Walmsley building a paper making machinery factory. The new Astley Bridge Police Station was also built on part of the sports field. Although it bears the name Astley Bridge, it is in Tonge Moor. The north west corner of this land was used as a cinder tip, and after the war I believe a company from Wigan bought the tip and removed most of the cinders. The site was taken over by North West Water as a depot, however they moved on and the land was used for a new housing estate.

From the meeting of the two brooks we go west along Astley brook, to our left was the North End Spinning Mill No 2, built in 1903. It closed in 1963. Reopening as Automotive Products and finally closing in 1985. The site is now occupied by Waters Meeting Health Centre.

(North End No1 mill was in Canning Street.)

On the opposite side of the brook were a sewage works, brick works and also some allotments. We are now back to just short of Blackburn Road. On our left was the site of Astley Bridge Railway Station, which opened 15th October 1877. There was talk of the line coming into the village proper; however the cost of crossing the ravine stopped that development.

Due to lack of demand the station closed 1st October 1879. Unfortunately although there were eight trains a day to and from Bolton the trains only averaged 5 people a journey. The tram system was more convenient as people could get on a tram near their home and get off at numerous stops in the town centre. The line became just a goods and coal depot. By 1961 according to Bill Simpson the goods yard became a storage area for condemned wagons. Finally the yard closed in 1964.

McDonalds now stands on some of the site. There is a Public house on each side of the Astley Bridge. The Tippings Arms to the south and the Bridge to the north with the Railway Hotel, whose original name was the Church Inn just a little, further up Blackburn Road. Across from what was the railway goods yard stood Cosy Fires the trade name of J& J Scholes a well known coal merchant in the district. In front of their building was a weighbridge. The southern boundary of Astley Bridge as defined by Mr Archibald Sprake is Astley Brook, any buildings or areas below the brook are not in Astley Bridge although in some newspapers and magazines such buildings as All Souls Church or the Valley School are referred to as being in Astley Bridge.

22

THE OLD ROAD TO BLACKBURN

Having gone around the Astley Bridge boundary the size of the village is 1761 acres

Proceeding north over Astley Bridge, on the west side there were six premises before Kelly Row. First of the six was a provision dealer and the last of the six was a grocer. These buildings stood where the snooker hall now stands.

Kellys Row was renamed Viola Street, and has a short row of stone cottages which are some of the oldest in the village. The Street leads to an industrial estate.

Severe thunderstorms hit Astley Bridge in 1950; these storms were the worst for many years. Blackburn Road was closed as part of a wall collapsed near the Railway Hotel. All essential services were cut including telephones, gas, electricity, and water. In the early 50s a gas main broke just a few yards up Blackburn road than the Railway Hotel.

Way back in 1875, Old Road had a sewer collapse, and there have been other incidents of flooding in the village. On 18th July1964, a storm said to be the most in tense ever recorded in Bolton hit the area, and between 9-15 and 11am 2.8 inches of rain fell. The heavy rain began on the Friday and in the 2 days 4.7 were recorded. Hundreds of homes and factories were flooded and a 15 feet crater appeared just off Old Road. It was just about at the entrance to ASDA car park near the HSBC Bank. Most likely it was the result of what would be a small brook running below what was Lee Clough.

In 1978 a sewer collapsed and a twenty feet cavern was found near the Bridge Inn

On the opposite side of Blackburn Road was a mixture of dwellings with Heywood's Hollow and Knowles Court dividing them. Astley Bridge Reform Club was in the next block together with a number of businesses, newsagent, clogger, butcher, green grocer, followed by the Manchester and County Bank, and next door was the Craven Heifer. With two more shops to Seymour Road.

On the opposite side of the road on the corner of Viola Street was a greengrocers, probably most of us would remember Robert Price, the plumbers being there. Next is the archway to Back Kelly Row, then came The Foresters Arms which closed sometime in the 1890s, Bretherton's taxis took the premises followed by a row of stone cottages which are there today and meet Waverley Road, which was originally called Astley Lane. Probably named after "Astley House" which was on the lane, and incidentally belonged at one time to James Eden (Eden's orphanage) and later by William Harper (a trustee of the orphanage) When the street was renamed, the lane passing the cemetery still retained the Astley name although it was known locally as Skrike Fowt. In fact in the 1871 census it is shown as Skrike Fold.

The story goes that a Scotsman, Alexander Macdonald lived in one of these cottages got into financial difficulties, he decided to end it all by cutting his throat, and he ran out of his cottage brandishing a cut throat razor, skriking "Bury me where I let".

The story goes on to say that many years later, some workmen were repairing the road when they dug up a coffin bearing the initials A.M.

Facing the row of cottages is the cemetery whose first internment was 16th October 1884. The Chapel was built in 1883 and is a grade two listed building, covering eight acres. The land was originally part of Battersby's Farm

The Astley Bridge Local Board formed in 1864 bought the land from Eden Trust. There are separate areas for Anglicans, Catholics and Dissenters.

ASTLEY BRIDGE CEMETARY CHAPEL

The Chapel is a Grade 2 listed building which was designed and intended to serve all Christian denominations. There are 47 war graves of people serving in both world wars. There has been 18,767 burials since October 1884 till May 2012 according to Bolton Council records. At the entrance of the cemetery is a plot where we find Gypsy graves.

For many years before the opening of the cemetery this area of Astley Bridge was a favourite wintering spot for the Gypsy people. Consequently it was felt right to allot space for their departed. Facing the bottom of Thorns Road is a short stretch leading to the gate of the cemetery. At the entrance is a number of Gypsies

Graves, many of which have quite imposing, and grand headstones. It was reported in the Bolton Evening News dated 21st July 1965 that the Romany funeral of Mr Isaac Frederick Bird there were between 60 and 80 cars, 150 mourners from all over the country. The grave was tiled in glazed bricks the cost of grave and headstone was £2,000.

An interesting fact although nothing to do with Astley Bridge, was reported in the Journal & Guardian on 2nd April 1953 about the cost of Charlotte Crompton's funeral on 12th August 1866 She was buried at Lever Bridge church. Funeral charges, as follows.

Digging Grave at 1/2 per foot- 8 Feet	9/4
Total cost of new ground	10/-
Clergy	2/-
Clerk	1/-
Bell	1/-
Bier and carriage	1/-
Total	£1/4/4
Plus	
Headstone	5/-
Admission fee for Sexton	1/-
Sexton fixing headstone	1/-

Astley Lane finally finishes in Sharples Vale which is one of those small industrial areas found dotted around the town. Before the coming of the industrial revolution this must have been a very beautiful spot with Astley Brook coming down the valley which would be covered in trees and bushes, but unfortunately it is a different story today. The old cobbled road from Astley Bridge to Halliwell has been closed off just after

Skrike Fold, and has now been taken over by nature. The only entrance to the Vale is from Raglan Street. The mills and the row of cottages (Sharples Vale Cottages) backing onto the brook have all gone. It is amazing how many organisations used the mills and buildings over the last 200 or so years.

SHARPLES MILL 1902

WILLIAM WALTER CANNON

William Walter Cannon together with R M Haslam (another big Bolton cotton baron) became Cannon and Haslam, operating Sharples mill 1843-53.

William Walter Cannon

Born 16th November 1822

Died Hill Cot 19th June 1903

Mayor 1871-73

Emma his wife Mayoress

Brother in law Richard Stockdale Mayor 1864-66

Alderman 1854-56 & 1872

Magistrate

Registrar Leigh County Court

Clerk of the peace, Bolton 1878

Mayor on opening of New Town Hall 1873

Freeman of the Borough 6th September 1899

Vice President of Bolton Cotton supply Organisation.

It appears that the mill was possibly rebuilt in the early 1880s, and in 1884 James Brimelow, Cotton Spinners, started business there, followed in 1887 by Greenhalgh and Shaw's. By 1900 John Schofield a waste spinner and wadding manufacturer had taken over the building.

In 1821 in an adjacent building was a bleachworks started by Nightingale and Southworth, then Eden and Thwaites followed by various members of the Murton family. The "Townsman" or as we would say today "Representative" during some of this time was the father of Sir Arthur Rostron, the Captain of the steamship Carpathia, Other businesses in the building were Messrs Watson and Openshaw (foundry), then Maxilin Mint Company who bought medicated confectionary in bulk and then packing them into smaller packet. There was also the Vale Freezing Company producing tubular ice lollies in for different flavours. One company made parts for the Bond Mini Car.

On the site were a gate house, a little hall, and the Mill Managers cottage which is still there, although the belfry has been removed from the roof.

James Frederick Riley became assistant manager in 1871 at the age of 18 and by 1881 he became manager.

JAMES FREDERICK RILEY

Born 18th November 1852 in Eagley
Died 7th June 1911
Married to Harriet Holt, 13th May 1874 at St. Paul's Astley Bridge.
4 Children
1891 became manager of cotton mill in Preston
1901 became manager of cotton mill in Settle

Going back to the thirties it was common practice for mills and factories to sound their hooters when it was time to start work, at say 7-30 a.m. Hooters would be blowing all over the town. Should you be on your way to work when the hooter sounded, you were late and probably be quartered, meaning that if you were 2 minutes, or more late you would lose a quarter of an hours pay.

The bell in the belfry on the manager's cottage was like the hooters. It was to warn people that the mill or factory was starting.

There is a story the Mr Midgley at one time the Managing Director of Greenhalghs went out to California. Some years later he returned to find that the bell had fallen down. He took it back to America and it is now hanging in a chapel there.

In the 1940s Messrs Smethust and Betney ran an engineering company repairing and making textile machinery. The Textile and Accessory Repair Company On a shelf in a small office stood rows of spindles, the variety was amazing even to the seasoned mill worker some of the spindles would be a mystery. However the factory was more than capable of manufacturing all of them. Such as "Gassing Spools" or what about "Copskewers", or for good measure "Throstlewinders".

On the eastern side of the cemetery was the site of Astley Bridge Wanderers football ground complete with a grandstand which would be quite something in those days as league football was in its infancy, and to have a grandstand could have been a bit of a novelty. In its day the club was in competition with what are now Football League Clubs. The club was formed in the late 1870s playing in the Lancashire cup on 11th October 1879 winning 6 -0 against Blackburn Rising Sun, they beat Blackburn Christ Church in the next round 2-1, but for some reason they did not play in the 3rd round. On the 6th October 1883 they lost to Newton Heath LYR club 1-0. in the Lancashire Cup. Newton Heath were formed by employees of the Lancashire & Yorkshire Railway Company. The club eventually changing their name to the world famous Manchester United.
The Lancashire Football Association was formed by a meeting held at the Volunteer in Bromley Cross on Sunday 28th September 1878.

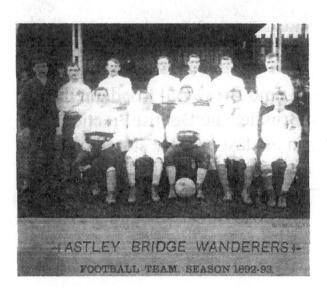

ASTLEY BRIDGE WANDERERS

Some time around the turn of the 20th century the club folded. I
do not know the reason unless the land was bought by a builder.
Ashbee Street and Bloomfield Street now stand on the site.
Astley Bridge Football was reborn around 1930 playing on land
previously used by Astley Bridge Cricket Club who had to find
a new venue, because a new road was being built from Tonge
Moor to Astley Bridge, namely Crompton Way the construction
of which sliced about a third of the cricket ground away. The
reduced sized ground was an ideal spot for the newly formed
football club.

Back to the start of Lamb Brow/Old Road, on the left are a
number of houses, Brindles the Dentist Practice was in one of
them with a joiner in the last one. He stored timber in the yard at
the side of the house, and 60 years ago timber was left to
weather for a couple of years before being used. A similar yard
could be found in Primrose Street belonging to the Arrowsmiths.

ASTLEY BRIDGE BAPTISTS

THE ORIGINAL BAPTIST CHAPEL AND SUNDAY SCHOOL

ASTLEY BRIDGE BAPTIST CHAPEL AS IT IS TODAY

As you entered Eden Street in the late 1800s on the right hand side was a bowling green followed by The Baptist Chapel. As far as we know the first Baptist Chapel was in King Street and was used sometime before 1796 (Rev J R King, Baptist Beginnings in Bolton) Things were not going well and the chapel was closed and sold in 1806.

Some 11 years later it was decided to plant a church in Bolton. Two students from the Baptist College at Horton, Bradford, were sent to Bolton on 27th June 1819. They had a letter of introduction which they took to Mr John Lum a trustee of the old King Street Chapel. Unfortunately he declined to assist in any attempt to help the Baptist cause. However there were some active Baptists in the town and St Andrews Presbyterian Church, commonly known as the Scotch Church which stood where St Paul's now stands at the end of Deansgate. The church had been put up for sale. The Scottish Presbyterians due to lack of numbers had returned to Dukes Ally.

The Baptists managed to rent the building as a temporary measure for an annual ground rent of £25 per year. The church was opened as a Baptist Chapel in May 1819.

In 1832 the Rev Wm Fraser started a weekly evening service in the home of Ralph Leach. There were no places of worship in Astley Bridge village at that time. Whilst there was a school records about the school are virtually non existent.

In 1836 Ash Grove owned by Mr Garnett Taylor was rented by the Baptists Sunday for worship and for two years all went well, then people turned up as usual for their Sunday Service only to find the doors of the building locked.

The owner of the building said that it was going to be used as an Anglican School. Anglicans started to worship there prior to moving into the new St Paul's Church.

The Methodists bought Ash Grove for £200 in 1853. By 1854 they had 41 boys and 55 girls together with 332 scholars and 31 officers. They sold the building in 1864 for £240.

The Baptists then went back to the main Chapel on Moor Lane, which incidentally was built whilst the Baptists worshipped at the Scotch Church, where St Paul's Deansgate now Stands.

The Astley Bridge Baptists were certainly resilient as they opened a Sunday school the same year, 1838, in Eden Street with 80 Scholars attending.

The chapel was built in 1861 with seating for 450 people. Looking at old photographs, there appears additional building at a later date, possibly in 1846. In the Sunday school was a library containing 1,432 books. It had a Sick and Burial Society, a Tract Society, a Band of Hope, and a Temperance Society. Eventually over the years and falling attendances the old Chapel and Sunday school became a liability, and in the 1970s the Chapel and Sunday school were demolished with part of the land being sold to Anchor Housing.

On the rest of the site a new smaller modern Chapel was built. In the early days of the chapel there was a bowling green on the Old Road side, but I have not been able to find out about whose bowling green it was, it may have belonged to the Baptist church but have no proof of this and it is now part of the churches car park has long since gone and is now part of the churches car park.

Eden Street continues up the hill to the Cemetery gates. By the looks of the road surface the top half of Eden Street which was known in the 1800s as Stable Brow has not been adopted by the town and lacks maintenance.

ENTRANCE TO ASTLEY BRIDGE CEMETARY

OLD ROAD

In Astley Bridge's early days Old Road and Berkeley Road were featured in bringing Christianity to the village that was before the present religious denominations built their churches and chapels. There were at least two mission halls, plus Berkeley Hall, together with the people's mission room at number 51 in two face row.

At the top of Berkeley road was a church house which became a mission hall for the Brethren church in 1919. Lee Clough was a popular place for Christian tent meetings with many evangelists coming to preach the word,

We go back to Lamb Brow to continue our journey on the old Blackburn Road. At the start of the Brow stands the Lamb Hotel which is one of the two oldest in the village the other being the Lawson's arms (Three Pigeons). At the back of the Lamb was a small area known as Tantrum Barracks. This was quite a special place, as if people did not "see eye to eye" or needed to sort each other out, they would go to the back of the Lamb and have a set too.

Opposite the Lamb Hotel on the Brow, stood one of the many Co-op shops found in Astley Bridge. As we progress up Old Road to the right we pass a terrace of seven houses including a shop, then Back Argyle Street followed by another pub The Levers Arms. In a photo showing Old Road the Levers Arms has an advertisement showing "Booths Home Brewed" on its gable end. Next door is a double fronted house which in 1887 Street Directory shows it as The Rifle Volunteer Beer house, followed by Argyle Street, behind is Back Lee Clough Street then a few more houses comes Diamond Row. Before we get to the Edge Tavern there was Mission Hall but who met there is a bit of a mystery

Back Lee Clough Street and Diamond Row became quite run down. Tom Benson tells us that they inhabited with mainly Irish labourers probably attracted there by low rents, and jobs helping to build the mills.

At what is now the entrance to Asda car park stood a mission hall, probably called the Berkeley Hall maybe that is why Berkeley Road was so named. It is funny how the past repeats it self as roughly on the same spot now stands Lee Clough Mission. Well before the building of Asda and prior to that Hesketh's Mills, and reservoir was Lee Clough valley which ran from just short of what is now Moss Bank Way down to Diamond Row.

In the Clough was a stream which I believe originated somewhere in the Barlow Park/Oldham's area.

Heskeths mill lodge was probably built out of part of the valley and the little brook flowing through finished in the Lodge. The overflow from the lodge possibly takes itself into the original brooks course. One wonders if the brook was culveted nearly 200 years ago.

Some 300 years ago this valley would have been a scene of beauty with trees and plants in abundance and the bubbling stream running through.

Lee Clough was affectionately known as't tip. At some time in the past, debris was tipped into the valley which was some thirty feet or so lower than Old Road. The Edge Tavern could have been given the name because it was on the edge of the tip. Tucked in at the northwest end of the valley between lodge and the mill was Ash Bank/Grove, which was a terrace of five houses. It was here where the Baptist church started to put its roots down in the village. There is also some reference to a school prior to St Paul's but its whereabouts has been lost to antiquity. There could be at least three possibilities. Ash Grove, Berkley Hall which could have been, or became a scout hut, or The peoples Mission Room at number 51 Old Road.

THE TIP, OR LEE CLOUGH VALLEY

The Tip in its time was a recreation area for the village, and whilst it wasn't as big as say Astley Bridge Park it could be said that it was a sort of village green. At the north end of the valley nestling between Heskeths mill lodge and the service building is a row of buildings known as Ash Bank. Some older maps show a clutch of buildings in front of Ash Bank which were demolished time at the turn of the 20th century. The tip certainly was well used before the park was opened early in the twentieth century. Circuses, Fairs complete with coconut shies, carousels, and the odd side show. Markets were held here. Evangelists and Rechabites pitched their tents here. It was used at times as a camping site for Gypsies, their piebald ponies and caravans. When not being used for these things it was a great place for children. Football, Cricket, Rounders, Piggy and many other children's games were played on't tip.

On the Old Road side was a rise of some 30 feet from the Clough bottom to Old Road. The man made rise was mostly made up of tipped ash and cinder waste from a mills boiler fires. This hill was ideal for sledging in winter, and in summer children would sit on any old tray or sheet of metal and slide down the cinder screed from top to bottom.

Before the coming of ASDA the first Lee Clough Mission building stood on Penny Brow, which was a road down t'tip. The road went alongside Hesketh's mill wall on one side and on the other were some buildings including the Mission. The old Lee Clough Mission closed its doors after 70 years at the end of March1965. The mission was started from an adult Bible class from Seymour Road Methodists. On its closure the congregation went back to the Methodist Church staying there until the new chapel was built for around £10.000. Furniture from the old chapel was stored in the basement of the Seymour Road Church.

LEE CLOUGH MISSION

The new Chapel was built on a location on Old Road where a number of buildings had stood many years before. Sadly the Mission held it last service on 30th December 2012 and the building has been put up for sale.
Many other properties in the area were demolished around the turn of the twentieth century.

PENNY BROW OR PENNY SCHOOL BROW

In the mid eighteen hundreds very few people could read or write, and usually if a child went to Sunday school for forty-eight weeks of the year it won a prize which in most cases was a Christian book or Bible. Unfortunately the prizes were in a sense useless, because the majority of people in those days could not read or write and churches up and down the land decided to overcome the problem by giving lessons after church or Sunday school. In many cases the lessons were free but some churches charged a penny a session. There is some uncertainty how Penny Brow got its name as records are uncertain whether the little Mission Chapel on Old Road, charged a penny to people who could afford to pay, or as I have already said that there is some evidence of a school in the area who may have charged a penny per pupil for a day or maybe more days teaching. It seems reasonable Penny Brow or Penny School Brow got its name maybe, first as a nick name, where people said they were going to the penny Chapel or Penny school, and from that the Brow got its name.

When ASDA got the land where Heskeths mills stood, the Chapel and other private properties were bought so the land could be used to build a bigger car park.

Unfortunately for ASDA one person would not sell his property which stood on the corner of Blackburn Road and Penny Brow for quite a good number of years. Eventually they managed to buy the property and immediately moved the petrol station from the Old Road exit to its present Blackburn Road site.

ASDA started business in Astley Bridge on19th May 1970. In those days there was a restaurant a DIY department which sold timber. Some years ago the store was altered and the restaurant and DIY have gone making the store much different one that opened in 1970

Historically, Lee Clough Tip up to the 1950s was the heart of Astley Bridge, being a convenient centre of activities and surrounded by St Paul's, Seymour Road Methodists, Baptist, St Anthony's and Holy Infants churches, and also at a little later date the Gospel Hall. The only exception to these denominations was the Congregation (now U R C chapel) at Bank top which was a bout a mile away.

Starting on the other side of Old Road from Eden Street was the Co-op, houses , Longworth Court, a couple more houses then Taylor's Court, The next row of houses is known quaintly as "Two Face Row" the reason being, is, with each couple of houses the front doors come together and over each door is a face. These mouldings face each other.

In this row at Number 51, around the turn of the twentieth century was The Peoples Mission Room, so far I have been unable to find out for what it was used. Maybe it was an annex to Berkely Hall. We now arrive at the bottom of Thorns Road;

facing is Dandy Row cottages, and here Old Road Becomes Berkely Road. Next are a couple of cottages facing south with more properties behind them including a "church house" but which church? This is shown on some maps as a Mission Hall. In 1919 the Brethren church in Astley Bridge moved from meeting in Mr and Mrs Martins in Dormer Street to rent a hall in Berkeley Road at 5/- per week. Was this the mission hall? And as we come to what is now Moss Bank Way we pass a Scout Hut. All the buildings from the two cottages have been demolished. On the corner of Old Road and Cavendish Street was a flat post box let into the wall.

Returning to Thorns Road, which was possibly known in the past as "Road to the Thorns." Just before the road got to "The Thorns" there was a large private development being Eden's Orphanage. Founded by James Eden of Eden and Thwaites Bleachworks, which was at Waters Meeting on the boundary of Bolton and Astley Bridge.

JAMES EDEN AND THE ORPHANAGE

James Eden was born in Blackburn and was the main partner of Eden and Thwaites Bleachworks. He was quite a wealthy man with houses at Showley Hall in Clayton-Le-Dale. Fairlawn in Lytham, and as I have already said Astley House in Astley Bridge. James was never married however he was greatly involved in Poor Law Union, and Chairman of the Conservative Registration Society.

He also became a Magistrate of Lancashire 16th October 1850. James Eden died peacefully in his sleep 23rd April 1874 age78. His housekeeper went to make a fire in his bedroom, as she did each day. James appeared to be asleep however when she went into his bedroom a second time she realised that things were not right and he had passed away. It was reported that he was a well loved member of the Lytham community, and many people's blinds were drawn and flags were flown at half mast on many buildings on the day of his funeral.

In his will he made a bequest of £10,000 for the building of an orphanage in Astley Bridge, plus an endowment fund of £40,000 making a magnificent total of £50,000. In the terms of the will was for the care, support and bringing up of destitute orphans and infant children whose parents at the time of death dwelt within the area of the Bolton Poor Law Union.

An area of land of 4acres,I rod, and 21 perches were purchased from part of Taylors Tenement Farm, and a Board of Trustees and Governors were appointed. These were quite powerful and wealthy men with great experience in the commercial field.

Board of Trustees for Eden's Orphanage

Thomas Thwaites, Bleacher of Watermillock
William Harper, of Astley House
James Knowles Mill Owner of Eagley Bank
John Ashworth, Mill Owner of Ollerton
Thomas Wilkinson of Whitehill
William Tristham, Cotton manufacturer of High Lawn

T M Hesketh, Mill Owner of Summerfield
James Barlow, Mill Owner (Barlow and Jones) of Greenthorne
Edgworth. And The Mayor and ex-Mayor (For the time being,)
whatever that meant

JAMES BARLOW

He was married to Alice
He was a councillor for Bradford and West Wards,
An Alderman for Derby Ward and also the Mayor of Bolton
1867-69.
Chairman of the Parks Committee, advocating that parks should
be opened on Sundays.
President of Bolton Mechanics Institute
Founder of the Institute of the Workshops for the Blind
Was involved with his brother in the YMCA
A Magistrate from 1858
A life long temperance campaigner. And was against workhouse
girls being sent to work in Public houses.
He opened Lark Street Temperance Hall 1860.
Bolton Moor Temperance Hall 1869.
Bolton's first non alcoholic pub the Barlow Arms on Bridge
Street on 26th November 1877 followed by the Bolton Arms on
Bradshawgate.

42

He also proposed the adoption of the Public House Closing Act
(where public houses closed from 1am to 5 am) which was
passed by the Bolton Council)
A Methodist Sunday School teacher
Laid Foundation Stones for Higher Bridge Street Primitive
Methodist Church,
St Mark's Fletcher Street,
Mawdesley Congregational Church Great Moor Street,
Claremont Baptist Church St Georges Road,
together with Edgworth Wesleyan Chapel.
He gave the estate and donated £5,000 maintenance of the
Children's Home at Crowthorne Edgworth. Known as Barlow
Memorial Home.
On1stAugust 1873 he unveiled the statue of Dr Samuel Taylor
Chadwick another generous philanthropist.
His son Sir Thomas Barlow became physician to Queen
Victoria, King Edward 7th, and King George the 5th.

His daughter Annie Barlow is another revered Boltonian. As an
expert in Egyptology she spent a lot of time in that land Annie
donated many of the exhibits in Bolton's Egyptology
Department. Which is noted as one of the best outside London.

His grandson Sir James Alan Noel Barlow married a
granddaughter of Charles Darwin.

The orphanage was situated on Thorns Road in Sharples Park it
was a handsome building was opened in 1879. The building is
148 feet long and 48 feet deep. The building originally had a
tower, however during some alteration it was thought wise to
take the tower down. The structure had two wings. Upstairs
were two large dormitories one for boys and one for girls, and
smaller dormitories for senior scholars, and also bedrooms and
bathrooms for schoolmistresses and servants. On the ground
floor there were rooms for the matrons and schoolmistresses.

The two wings were connected by dining room and kitchen. Over these were nine classrooms. However I feel that these were used less and less as numbers dwindled and eventually the children went to local schools. The two attics were set aside for hospital needs, however eventually a hospital was built in the grounds.

Swimming baths and washhouses were provided with both covered and open playgrounds complete with swings.

Large gardens both vegetable and landscape. Over the years hundreds and hundreds of local children passed though its doors, however with Widows and Orphans Pension Act and children's allowances the need for this type of institution diminished.

By1948 a third of the house was taken over by Greenhalgh and Shaw as a nursery.

In 1950 it was decided to sell the building and use the money for a smaller place near the sea.

In 1951 it was taken over by the Independent Isis School, however it became too expensive to run and Isis moved out in 1966.The building was sold and demolished to make way for private development.

The gatehouse which itself is very handsome building is the only part of the project still standing proudly bearing the carved stone sign EDEN ORPHANAGE 1878 embellished with carved branches and animals.

44

THE THORNS

This was one of the oldest houses in the village till its demolition in 1965. The Thorns was quite a large house with 3 cottages attached, the area was known as Thorns Fold. Was the fold named after the house, or was the house named after the fold?

One of its first residents was a John Yates shown as a Rumworth Yeoman, he lived there in 1797, by 1841 the census shows that John and Mary Hardcastle lived there John was part of the banking family of Thomas Hardcastle who together with James Cross, James Ormrod, Robert Barlow, and Thomas Rushton formed the first commercial bank in Bolton. It was known as Hardcastle Cross and company.

The bank issued its own notes from 1821, and the Bolton News reported 2nd May 2012 that a black and white banknote produced when Bolton printed its own money sold at auction for £900. The note was about 150 years old. The note was a proof and never issued consequently it was in very fine condition. The note shows the names of the five Bolton businessmen who formed the bank, Hardcastle, Cross, Ormrod, Barlow, and Rushton.

The Bolton Bank existed from 1818 to 1879, and then it became Manchester and Salford Bank, later Williams and Deacons, Williams and Glynnes, and finally Royal Bank of Scotland. The banks handsome building is on the corner of Market Street and Deansgate.

In 1861 the census shows a William Tristham who was a Cotton Weaver Manager employing 450 workers living at the Thorns. Followed by1871 John Ashworth, 1881 Mary Conway, 1891 Sarah E Scowcroft. The house was then bought by Emily Plethean no dates available.

In 1918 Arthur Sandaver Holmes and his family of Ashleigh moved to the Thorns. Arthur was a J P for 31 years, and was Church Warden at St Pauls Astley Bridge. He gave an oak table, to the glory of God and to the church as a thankful acknowledgement of 25 years of happily family life. I believe that the table is on the north side of the church.

There is also a window given to the glory of God and in the church in memory of Arthurs service. This window was erected by his wife family and friends.

On the death of his father 30th July 1943, Cyril Butler Holmes and family took over the house. C B was a fine athlete competing in the Olympic Games in Berlin in 1936 in the 100 and 200 metres. Unfortunately he did not win but made up for it in the 1938 Empire Games by winning both the 100 and 200 metre titles. He also played three times for England at Rugby Union. In the 1936 games he wore a pair of Fosters running shoes which were so light they only lasted for one race.

In 1952 C B died and the property was turned over to his widow Ada Elizabeth Holmes who sold it to Harry Markland a retired butcher who developed the land for housing in 1965.

Coop Street starts at Berkely Road running up to the area known as the Park. It is quite a long terrace of 23 houses on the west side with just 6 on the other side one of the unusual things about the street is the last 4 houses in the long terrace have front gardens.

The Park was an area taking in Park Avenue and a number of houses and gardens which were partly demolished for the new Moss Bank Way opened in 1938. Moss Bank Way is part of what was going to be a ring road around the town this particular length was about two and a half miles linking Victoria Road/Old Kiln Lane junction with the Blackburn Road/Crompton Way junction, at a cost of some £93,699. At the top of Halliwell Road a number of houses were demolished also the tram terminus was moved. The road continues towards Astley Bridge crossing a stone arched bridge up the hill and unfortunately the Holmes family lost a piece of their land, as did Astley Bridge Cricket

Club whose dressing rooms had to be relocated because they were in the path of the new road.

ASTLEY BRIDGE CRICKET CLUB

The cricket club has had a pretty chequered career. It started life as Halliwell Cricket Club and for some 60 years played at Bennett's, a piece of land bordering on what is now Bennett's Lane and Elgin Street. The club were founder members of Bolton and District Cricket Association in 1889. Unfortunately the land was sold for building development and the club had to look elsewhere for a ground. They finally found some land in the Cobden Street area of Astley Bridge.

By this time the large service reservoir facing houses in Holland Street had been drained and built on. The club still played as Halliwell until 1921 when they officially became Astley Bridge. Cobden Street passed between two gable ends passing some hen pens and then came the new cricket ground.

Disaster struck the club again, as the new Ring Road which opened as Crompton Way in 1928 chopped a fairly big slice of the ground.

The Cricket Club were on the move again. The Club found some land for relocation at Sharples Park; however the ground needed a lot of work to make it fit for cricket so the club temporarily moved to a pitch off Belmont Road. Work began in earnest and the Bolton Journal dated 15th October 1926 tells us that there were some allotments on the land which had to move and the area was cleared ready to prepare the ground. Some of the best turf was brought from Cobden Street for the wicket. Len Tubbut the clubs professional was in charge of the programme and by 1930 it had moved to its present Sharples Park ground. Another blow hit the club at the construction of Moss Bank Way when as already said a slice of the pitch was taken by the new road which opened in 1938. The club continued to play at Sharples Park on a much smaller area.

Adversity seemed to follow the club as the grounds landlords, the Bleachers Association decided to sell the land. The price was £3,200, the clubs members together with local people and businesses rallied round and the money was found to the great relief of many Astley Bridgeites. I understand that Thornleigh College were interested in the land for future development. However, maybe the Cricket Club being sitting tenants had first refusal.

Most of this information is from reports from the club.

The present cricket ground is flanked on the west side with what the locals call the Mile o' Boards which is a slight exaggeration of a high boarded fence which ran from around the top of Thorns Road towards Moss Lea a little knot of houses not too far from Moss Lea Farm. A road come footpath takes you through Blue bell Wood passing on your right some Moss Lea council allotments, down too, and over a jiggling footbridge crossing Astley Brook to Temple Road.

Retracing our steps we make our way towards the junction of Oldhams Lane and Sharples Park and on our left we pass a narrow lane leading to Harricroft Farm, or as it is known today as Smithills Open Farm. It has many kinds of farm animals as well as animals from far afield such as lamas and alpacas. Just northwest of the farm is Tippet House, a listed building. Whilst Tippet House is in Astley Bridge the only way to it by road is from Smithills Dean Road.

BARLOW PARK

Going east, and alongside Harricroft farm is Barlow Park The Park was originally built by the Directors of Barlow and Jones as a recreation area for their employees the Playing Fields and were opened on 20th August 1927.

The playing fields were magnificent, covering 23 acres of land. They contained

5 tennis courts

3 Bowling greens

2 Hockey Pitches

2 football pitches

1 cricket pitch

Together with a splendid pavilion with firs class changing rooms.

Whist the playing fields were first class, there was a problem not only with access but also was not very conveniently placed for Barlow and Jones workers, many of whom did not live locally. After about twenty years the company decided to give the playing fields to the town.

The Bolton Evening News on 23rd June 1950 reported that Sir Thomas Barlow conveyed the gift of the park to the Mayor (Alderman Mrs Wright) Sir Thomas said that "When they were planned, a great deal of thought and a considerable amount of money was put into their construction, and I hoped at the time that they would be very popular and would be used to the fullest possible extent." He then added "that he recognised that his company's employees might prefer their leisure and games in other parts of the town in association with other organisations and, that being so, his only desire now was that the playing fields should be fully used and enjoyed by others."

"There is" he says "undoubtedly a very great shortage of recreation grounds and playing fields in Bolton, and after considerable thought the board have decided on his recommendations to make the gift of Sharples playing fields to the town of Bolton for the benefit of the citizens at large to be used permanently." In conclusion, Sir Thomas expressed the hope that the park would remain as an open space, and would never be covered in houses.

Alderman Sykes Chairman of the Parks committee described the gift as truly magnificent when he expressed his thanks on behalf of the council and the people of Bolton.

Councillor Wood estimated that the gift, in money alone, was worth at least £50,000 to the people of Bolton.

HAYWARD LEIGH

Hayward Leigh was next door to Thornleigh in Sharples Park, and was a very desirable residence occupied by a number of local businessmen. In the 1887 directory there is an Edwin Woollard a bank manager living here. The census of 1891 shows Thomas Holmes and family living there, having lived previously at number 62 Seymour Road.

THORNLEIGH

Thornleigh House was built in1867-70 by Mr Arthur Lemuel Briggs born 1844 (a textile magnate) his wife was called Ellen Cordelia. The daughter of James Ormerod of Halliwell Hall. Their first son Christopher was christened on 11th November 1867. The St Paul's Parish Register shows Arthur's occupation as a Gentleman. He died in 1891 at the age of47.

John H Hargreaves of Hick Hargreaves bought the house. He died in 1903, his widow moved to Paignton, and the house was bought by Bolton Corporation in 1907 when it became a Women's Hostel. It closed in 1913. In 1914 it was fitted out as a hospital by Astley Bridge Red Cross, but later in1914 it became a refuge for Belgian refugees.

In 1919 it changed its use again becoming a hostel for disabled officers. On 29th October 1923 it closed. And was put up for auction being advertised as a, Desirable and Substantial Residence. It was sold at the Pack Horse Hotel for £4,000. Thornleigh had been bought on behalf of the Catholic Salasian Society to be used for a Catholic Secondary School for Boys.

In June 1925 a garden party had been organised to show and advertise the project to the Catholic community and about 1,000 people attended the event. I believe that the event was a total success as people were greatly impressed with the building and gardens.

On September 14th 1925 the school duly opened, and 44 boys including 13 boarders started Catholic secondary education in the town. By 1931 there were now 240 students including 45 boarders. A small farm near Thornleigh was purchased increasing the area of the ground to 12 acres. The College became co-educational in the 1970s

The Latin motto of the College is "Sicut Cervus" loosely translated "As the Hart" This was the motto of the Hargreaves family, and the head of the hart was on the family crest. The crest is worn on every student's blazer. I feel that the College have shown honour and respect to the Hargreaves family for not only retaining the Hargreaves family motto but also the house name as Thornleigh. Another slogan of the College is Engage, Enable, and Empower.

Some of Thornleighs notable former pupils.

Danny Boyle Oscar- winning film director.
Conor McGloion -   Guitarist in Kineses
Damon Gough -   Badly Drawn Boy.
Maurice Lindsley - Chairman Wigan Rugby League Club

Ian McAlister -   Chairman of Network rail
Helen Flanagan-actress
Frank Finley - actor.
Brian Finch – TV writer
Richard Henry McFarlane – poet known as Hovis Presley
Bernard Wrigley – Actor, comedian, and musician
Norman Prince – the Houghton Weavers
Tony Berry – Houghton Weavers.
Mike Pollitt Goalkeeper Wigan Athletic
Kerry Pollard   former MP
David Atherton - Founder of Dabs
Stuart Flinders BBC News reporter
Tom Parker Vocalist boy band The Wanted

THE LEES

Moving up Oldhams Lane we come to "The Lees" another
handsome house was occupied by Edward Thwaites in the early
1880s followed by William Musgrave iron founder and cotton

spinner. Then by Christopher Briggs, a Solicitor, and father of Arthur Lemuel Briggs of Thornleigh.

In 1935 "The Lees" was bought by Thornleigh and became living quarters for the Clergy Staff of the College, and has since the last war it has been extended. Both behind and in front of "The Lees" are extensive playing fields belonging to the College.

As we proceed on we come to Oldhams Council Estate built some time after the Second World War. The area got its name from a very small clutch of cottages, known as Oldhams Cottages and also Oldhams Farm nearby. These properties were quite isolated standing there on open, and at times wind swept moorland overlooking the town.

Samuel Crompton's family lived at the farm for eight years from 1782 to 1790 with the farm being in a secluded spot; he probably could enjoy some peace from near riots at Hall I'th Wood.

Samuel Crompton was born on 3rd December 1753 at Firwood Fold his father was a farmer. Whilst Samuel was a child his father died, but shortly before his death the family moved to Hall I'th Wood. His widow was a strong minded person. Well known for her delicious butter, honey, and elderberry wine. Samuels's uncle, Alexander Crompton also lived at the hall He was a remarkable individual. He was so disabled he could not leave his room where he worked on his loom weaving fusains. *As he was unable to go to church on Sunday he would listen* for the church bells ringing, then he would take off his working clothes and put on his Sunday best, then he would take his prayer book and read from the book for the length of the service including the sermon. He would repeat this later in the day for the evening service.

Samuel built his prototype Mule in 1779. As the Mule combined some of the features of James Hargreaves Spinning Jenny and Sir Richard Arkwright's Water Frame and as the Water Frame was patented, he was persuaded not to apply for a patent. Sadly this could have been the start of Samuels slide into poverty. Sir Robert Peel came to Oldhams to see Samuel with regard to the Mule and finances, but not a lot came from his visit. Had the Mule been patented Samuel Crompton would have been the equivalent of today's multi-millionaires.

His invention not only revolutionised the spinning industry, the Mule produced a finer and higher quality of yarn.

In 1790 he moved to King Street in Bolton. With his wife Mary (Pimlott) and his 3 sons and 1 daughter, by 1796 they had another 3 sons. Unfortunately Mary died in 1796. Samuel turned to his religion; he was a member of the New Jerusalem Swedenborgian church which was in Bury Street, Little Bolton. He was talented musician, playing his home made violin, writing hymns and he also built the chapel organ.

The church seemed to be off the beaten track, so to speak, with round about 40 worshippers each Sunday. The members had noticed that most of the churches in Little Bolton were bursting at the seams, All Saints, St. Georges, Bridge Street Methodists, All Saints, St Georges Road Congregational, St Georges Road Methodists, Claremont Baptists.

The Swedenborgians decided to move to a more central place, and built The New Jerusalem Chapel on Bridge Street which opened in 1844. It was reported at the time that at the first service held in the chapel it was full to overflowing, with many people unable to get in

Samuel died in poverty on 26th June 1827, leaving a wonderful legacy with his invention to the country. In 1823 a local group took pity on him and set up an annuity of £63/15/- for him. He was cared for by his daughter Betty until he died.

Bolton Library Archives tell us the following.

In 1811 Samuel Crompton toured the 650 cotton mills within a 60 mile radius of Bolton gathering evidence of how widely the spinning mule had been adopted, and he would use this information to partition parliament for some compensation.

Of the spindles used 155,880 were on the Spinning Jenny.
310,516 were on the water Frame, and 4,600,000were on the Mule.

Capitol invested in the cotton industry was worth around 40 million pounds. Tax paid to the Government was about £350,000 per annum. Around 80% of cotton goods bleached in the county was from Mule spun cotton.

Some 30 years had passed and Samuel had had little benefit from his invention, whist many mill owners had made fortunes from the Mule. It was recognised that he had given the Mule to the world for virtually nothing and parliament was ready to compensate him.

Mr Percival the Prime Minister was going to recommend a fair amount of compensation then bad luck struck. On 11th May 1812 Samuel was in the lobby of the House of Commons talking to Sir Robert Peel and Mr Blackbourne when Mr Percival the Prime Minister came along saying that he was going to propose compensation of £20,000.

Samuel Crompton probably full of joy and relief moved away and he was hardly out of sight when a mad man John Bellingham came up and shot the Mr Percival dead. He is the only Prime Minister to be assassinated. Samuel had to wait a further six weeks before his case was brought before parliament. On 24th June Lord Stanley moved that he should be awarded £5000.

Oldhams farm and cottages have now gone, and the Council have built an estate on the land. Then in 1954 Oldhams County Primary School was built, unfortunately the council closed the school because of lack of numbers of children coming through, and the pupils were sent to other primary schools in the area. Sadly after repeated arsonist attacks the council have decided to demolish the school.

Retracing our steps back down Sharples Park pass Thornleigh College we pass a number of quite large houses, one of which is Hyde Lea Nursing Home at number 49.

BROAD O'TH LANE

We make our way up the lane with Astley Bridge Park on our right, then about 100yards or so we cross a bridge although it isn't too easy to spot. 150years or so there was a ford in the road; however it was decided to bridge the stream. A lot of the local people said that it would be a waste of money as the water crossing the road was insignificant and a bridge was needless. The word needless stuck, for when the bridge was built the locals gave it the name of Needless, and the nickname stood, so much so that the name Needless Bridge appears on many maps. The correct name is Lees Bridge.

The lane, as the name suggests is not very wide and for most of its length is overhung by the trees on the edge of the park.

Many years ago Mrs Len Tubbut who was around 90 years old, told me that some where around where the bungalows stand on the north west border of the park, there was a stable where stage coaches from Bolton to Blackburn could change horses. Having researched the area I cannot find any references to the stables. However some old maps around 1850 show a Baptist Sunday School (chapel not built till 1861) at the top of an unnamed street running from Waverley Road which in those days was called Astley Lane.

Eden Street, again in those days only started at Taylor Street (now Lloyd Street) and ran north to the cemetery gates. The rest of Eden Street from Old road wasn't completed until around 1900. There were two ways to get to the original southern part of Eden Street. One was from Astley lane via Garnett Street and the other was from Taylor Street.

Again referring to old maps, one shows some buildings on the west side of what became the original Eden Street as being on Stable Brow. I wonder if these are the stage coach stables Mrs Tubbut was meaning as this was probably a secluded spot not far from the main road in which to change horses.

YEW TREE COTTAGE

As we continue up the lane we pass a drive which led to Yew Tree Cottage. According to the 1891 census, a Samuel R Chatwood and his family lived there. He was a safes work manager, and at the Paris Exhibition of August 1867 the English Engineers reported that Mr Chatwoods was the best safe in its capability in resisting burglars of appliances of any kind. James Kevan of P&J Kevan, Accountants 12 Acresfield lived there for a while. In May 1961 the company became Kevan Pilling & Co.

Another occupier of Yew Tree was William Nicholson who was a draper in Market Street. He was affectionately known as "Smiling Billy"

William Nicholson

Born 3rd February 1825
Died 29th November 1915

Son of Oliver Nicholson, ma member of Bolton's first Town
Council
Mayor of Bolton six times
Acting Caretaker Mayor on two occasions. Firstly for Benjamin
Alfred Dobson and secondly for John Edwin Scowcroft who
died in office.
He was the first Freeman of Bolton
Alderman
First President of Bolton YMCA
Chairman/Treasurer Committee Bolton Royal Infirmary
Governor of both Chadwick and Eden's Orphanages
President of Queen Street Mission
President of Bolton Certified Industrial School Lostock
Churchwarden St Georges connected with Church and Sunday
school for 63 years.
Chairman of the Watch Committee.

On 13th June 1907, aged 82, he was struck with a hammer by a
madman near Dobson's Statue in front of the Town Hall. He
was knocked to the ground and struck again several times. His
assailant was a quarryman named John W Ashton; he was later
judged as insane and sent to an asylum.
Some of the Yew tree property has gone and new buildings and
extensions have been created, with Yew Tree Cottage Care
Home is in this location.

At this point in the lane there are now bollards stopping the
traffic going any farther up the lane. These were put there to
stop people using the lane as a short cut to Belmont and
Blackburn Road. It seems ironic today as this was the original
way to both of the roads.
Facing are a number of bungalows, and I was told by a very old
resident many years ago that there were stables here where the
old stage coaches changed their horses.

Alongside the bungalows is a guinnel probably part of an ancient footpath which ran alongside the perimeter wall of what was a few years ago Openshaw's Mill which has long since been demolished. The mill site has been redeveloped and is now a private housing estate. This guinnel was a short cut to Maxwell Street, then on to Belmont Road.

Across from the guinnel is MacKenzie Street, its original name was West Street.

On this street are six Alms Houses. (The word Alms means "GIVEN FREELY TO RELIEVE THE POOR" The original Alms Houses were founded in 1839 by Mrs Lum The widow of Jacky Lum a religious manager of a mill and together with a board of trustees was formed to help oversee the project. This committee was created by three representatives from each of the following churches. Dukes Alley Chapel, Mawdesley Street Congregational, and Moor Lane Baptist.

The houses for poor widows were in Anchor Street off Folds Road. The houses were demolished to make way for a gasworks extension. The Corporation replaced them by building new Alms houses in MacKenzie Street, endowed by Mrs Lum.

The Journal and Guardian of 21st October 1949 goes on to say "It ruled the six houses should be kept in a good state of repair and furnished, and let free from rent and taxes to spinsters and widows above the age of 60, no more than two of whom should inhabit the same house."

There is a plaque over the centre of the buildings which reads-

"These Alms houses were founded in Little Bolton in 1839 By Mrs Lum for twelve poor widows and were transferred to this sit by Bolton Corporation Gas Department."

"Ald. Thomas Moscrop was the Chairman and they were opened on17th April 1886 by Ald. Joseph Musgrave and Thomas Fletcher the Mayor."

Back to Back with MacKenzie street is Cameron Street. On one side is a row of terraced houses and facing is Cameron Street Council Housing Estate.

The Estate covers 25 Acres containing 319 houses of various kinds and sizes. The original cost of each house and the weekly rent of each property are given in the following table.

Cameron Street Estate No 1   Built around 1934

4 Acres 58 Houses

8	850sf 3 beds £453	11/11
8	885sf 3 beds £468	11/11
24	863sf 2 beds £458	11/2
8	950sf 3 beds £496	16/1 plus parlour
10	920sf 3 beds £483	13/-

Cameron Street Estate No 2

21 Acres 261 Houses

40	772sf	3&4 beds	£404	10/2 11/5
18	779sf	3 beds	£407	10/2
88	756/752sf	2&3 beds	£368	8/3 9/9
25	767sf	3 beds	£400	10/2
36	682/699sf	2 beds	£367	8/3
18	785sf	3 beds	£410	10/6
12	322/425sf	1 bed	£290	4/9 6/- Bungalow
12	402sf	1 bed	£253	5/6 5/9 Flat
12	758/829sf	3&4 beds	£411	10/2 11/5

Virtually all the roads on both this estate and Oldhams have Scottish names. There does not seem to be any relevant reason why.

As we make our way to the end of Broad o'th Lane, we come to the junction of Belmont Road and Bar Lane to our left is a three story building affectionately known to the Astley Bridge villagers as the "Pepper pot" because of its shape. Crossing Belmont Road we go down Bar Lane passing on out left Ivy Bank Road where we find Astley Bridge Bowling Club, also in the road lived J H Hargreaves of Hick Hargreaves, he and his family lived in Beech House prior to moving to Thornleigh. St Paul's vicarage is also in the road, it is now the Old Vicarage Care Home.

Bar Lane continues down the hill to Blackburn Road.

Sir John Holden's Mill is quite a handsome and imposing red brick building dominating its side of Blackburn Road.

1940

SIR JOHN HOLDEN & SONS
LIMITED,

ORIGINAL DESIGN

SIR JOHN HOLDEN

Born 25th January 1862 in Raglan Street
Died 4th May 1926
Went to St. Paul's School Astley Bridge
Worked as A half Timer at Hesketh's mill
Went to evening classes to learn about all aspect of the cotton
industry at the Bolton's Church Institute
In 1885 he married Emma Caswell at St. Paul's Church Astley
Bridge.
They had eight children
1895 appointed manager at Firs Mill Leigh
Twice the Mayor of Leigh
1919 was knighted

On 13th April 1920 Lady Emma Holden cut the first sod on the
site of what was going to be the biggest cotton mill in the world.
It is a six storey building and some pent house apartments have
been erected on the roof.
Whilst I have no actual proof of this, but my father who saw the
mill being built from its foundations to finish, said that the mill
should have been built some two hundred yards or so from

Blackburn Road, however there was so much sand that the plans were changed.

There is a belt of sand roughly from Dunscar or thereabouts to Waters Meeting, and studying old maps we find there are many places marked as sand and gravel pits. Even moving the site, again my father told me that the concrete foundations were strengthened with hundreds of cotton skip tops and tons ballast. A great feature, or lack of one, is that there is no great mill chimney the mill would be driven by electricity.

The mill should have been twice the size, but the cotton industry was declining in Lancashire because India and other countries were starting to produce their own. Also the cost of the foundations were extremely high due to the sand, any further development was dropped. However it has to be said that it is a very smart building. Had the whole project been completed the second part of the mill would have been a reflection of the mill as it is, on the north side with the two towers side by side.

Again, had the whole planned mill been completed its output would have dwarfed probably any other cotton mill in the country, if not Europe as it would have had about 4 million spinning spindles.

1927

The architects of the mill were the well known Bolton Company of Bradshaw, Gass, and Hope. It is Bolton's oldest firm of architects which was established by Mr Jonas James Bradshaw in an office on Nelson Square in1862, and then in 1871 the company moved to19 Silverwell Street. Mr John Bradshaw Gass the nephew of the founder joined in 1882 and in 1892 Arthur John Hope joined the company.

One of their employees John Parkinson emigrated to North America, and after a number of jobs he settled in Seattle where he opened an architectural practice. He became quite successful being part of the team which designed the Los Angeles City Hall.

Los Angeles City Hall

During the war the copper covered dome of the Holden mill tower was painted black. This was a camouflage so that the German Bombers could not use it as a landmark. At the rear of the mill an area of land was fenced off for wartime allotments. These were to help the "Dig for victory" war effort.

Again at the rear of the mill was a fire escape, the bottom section had a counter weight meaning that as people came down this section the weight of the people would automatically help the steps to lower. As the steps emptied of people the counter weight would return the steps out of reach from the ground. However this did not deter the lads at the time of getting a tree branch with which to pull down the steps, and then make their way onto the roof of the mill. The mill was unique in Bolton, all the mills built previously in the town were driven by steam power whereas, Holden's mill used electricity to power the machinery, so there was no need for a tall chimney synonymous to other mills.

In those days the use of electricity as the main source of power was a bold step, as in the 1920s less than 10% of British homes were not wired for electricity. Could the electricity companies supply the increase demand for both homes and industry? Obviously Sir John was sure that they could. The main fuel in those days for lighting was gas.

The mill closed in 1965 and was taken over by Littlewoods Mail Order Company in 1985. Littlewoods closed their operation at the mill and in 2005 £9-5 million pounds project went ahead with the P J Livesey Group to completely refurbished the mill and it is now home to top quality highly desired apartments known as "The Cottonworks" Incidentally the group did a similar development at Eagley Mills starting in 1997.

At the same time the mill was being built the architects drew up plans for a vault to be built in Walmsley Church Yard at Egerton where the mills copper dome can be seen. It is built with Scottish Granite and inside is lined with Sicilian marble. At a cost of £4884/16/4. From the Vault the copper dome of Holden's mill could be seen.

Sir John died 4th May 1926 at Sharples Hall which he had renamed Ollerton Hall. In spite of the general strike which was paralysing the country 600 people attended his funeral. The coffin bearers were chauffeurs and gardeners from Sharples Hall. There were 126 wreaths surrounding the stone columns. B E N 13th May 1926. Sadly he died just before the mill was completed and running.

The original Sharples Hall stood at the north of the building until it was demolished probably in readiness for the rest of the mill to be built. This never materialised, and had it been built quite a large wooded area would have had to be cleared.

Through the wood was a cart track down to Sharples hall farm. Again like many farms this has gone and new houses have taken the farms place. The track to the farm has now been adopted and upgraded by the council, and is called Sharples Hall Fold.

The first house on Blackburn Road after Sharples hall Fold was one of the first, if not the first, to be built in Bolton after the last war. I believe it still has metal window frames synonymous with wartime buildings something of a rarity in these days.

On the corner of Bar Lane stands the Elms Nursery School at Numbers 717 and 719 at the latter Geo. Graveson a major ironmonger in the town lived for a number of years

The Brierfield Restaurant facing the mill was at one time a gentleman's house. Amongst its owners was Walter Mather, a cotton mill owner, Charles Scholes who was a director of Bury Road Colliery in Radcliffe, also Dr Faux a local GP.

Thornydyke Avenue runs alongside Briarfields.

Thornydyke Avenue takes its name from the house "Thornydyke" which was quite a large house with lots of land, sadly long since gone, and the land has been used for private house development.

"Thornydyke" was owned by the two mill owning brothers Nathaniel and Thomas Greenhalgh. Whilst they made their fortunes out of cotton spinning they had concerns for the spiritual sides of their workforce. It was reported in the Clutha Leader a New Zealand newspaper on 18th May 1877 that the late Nathaniel Greenhalgh had bequeathed £40,000 for the erection and endowment of two churches.

When Nathaniel died he left his fortune to his brother Thomas, who in turn set in motion the building of the first of the two churches. This was All Souls in Astley Street in 1878. It was consecrated by the Bishop of Manchester on 30th June 1881. The cost of building was £16,500; however the total cost which includes the school was just under £27,000.

Some interesting facts about All Souls.

Architects. Paley and Austin who also designed St Thomas's Halliwell. Whose parish All Souls is now in.

It has no official foundation stone at the request of Thomas Greenhalgh.

The church was lit by 12 gas pendants until 1929 when electricity was installed.

On 17th November 1966 it was united with St James in Waterloo Street

In 1987 it was vested in the redundant churches fund

The church was a warded a lottery grant to convert the building into a community centre.

The second church was The Saviours on Deane Road which opened in 1885, and sadly closed and was demolished in 1975. I understand that Thomas one Sunday went to church, and the theme of the minister's sermon was "Jesus the Saviour of all souls" after which the two churches were named.

Just alongside Thornydyke Avenue is a Toll house which stands proudly on its own. In 1797 Blackburn Road was a Turnpike road which started at the Lamb Inn going on its way to Blackburn, meaning that people had to pay to use the road.

I wonder if there was another Toll House on or near the site of the present one as this one wasn't built until around 1840.

TURNPIKE TRUSTS

These were bodies set up by acts of Parliament giving powers to collect tolls which would help to pay for the maintenance of the main roads. The term turnpike comes from the barrier used to prevent access; it was made from pikes being attached to cross members creating a gate, or toll gate. As the countries business grew, there were more and more horse and carts with much heavier loads, and other vehicles using the main roads which meant that they were becoming badly worn and rutted, requiring more and better maintenance.

The Act gave the trustees responsibility to maintain a particular stretch of road. Usually local clergy and businessmen were nominated as trustees, which incidentally were not paid but probably have the perk of not paying the toll when they were on the road.

The Act gave a maximum charge for the class of vehicle or animal using the road,

1/6 for a coach and four horses,

A penny for an unladen horse and

10d for a herd of 20 cows.

It became a common practice for trustees to auction off the lease to specialist Toll men who could enjoy some profit during the year. The length of turnpike covered by the Bolton to Blackburn trust was 15 miles. In 1846 the annual toll taken was £3998 but had dropped to £1185 by 1849. This was due to the completion of the Bolton to Blackburn railway.

During the last war two big six feet concrete cubes were placed on the pavements across from one another just higher up than the Toll Bar. There was just about enough room to pass on the wall side of them. Also close up to the wall again on the Toll bar side were up to 20 or more cylindrical blocks of concrete around 21 inches in diameter and roughly two feet six inches to three feet long. Should the Germans invade the round concrete blocks would be anchored across the road as a road block.

After the war the round blocks were not wasted many of them were used at Barrow Bridge as flood defences and can still be seen just at the bottom of the sixty three steps forming a strong bank to Dean Brook.

Next comes Thorncliffe Road, Stoneyhurst Avenue, and Sweetloves lane, have seen some house building since the war. Probably completing what was planned before the war started,

Our old road to Blackburn now takes us to Andrew Lane which was one of the four bus termini before and just after the war, the other two were Seymour Road, Dunscar and Eagley Way. Prior to the busses Astley Bridge was served by trams, Tram routes were not numbered. A letter was displayed on the front and rear of the tram. The letter to Astley Bridge was the letter **D** denoting Dunscar which was village's northern boundary.

The tram service was withdrawn on 4th October 1938.

The tram service started with Horse Trams on 1st September 1880, until 1st January 1900 when the first electric trams took over the route. Ron Horsley tells us about the first tram to run to Astley Bridge. He said, "There was a hitch when the driver forgot for a moment that the horse had to be steered on a predetermined track, and not cut corners he ran the cars wheels off the track for a yard or two. The error was soon remedied; the passengers had to get off the tram whilst the car was drawn back on the rails".

He also tells us that tram drivers were very poorly paid at 5d (2p) an hour. a total of £1/17/6 (£1-87p) for a 60 hour week.

B E N reported on 3rd February 1937 that Alderman Mrs Lawson argued the case for retaining Dunscar trams. Arguments against was that trams would be non-existent in 10 to15 years, also they took up the middle of the road, and the only difference between the trams at present was that the new trams had upholstered seats.

The bus numbers for the four Blackburn Road termini were

28 Seymour Road

29 Andrew Lane

30 Dunscar Bridge.

31 Eagley Way

10 Crompton Way terminus originally in Holland street

Another route coming through to Belmont was Number 5

At the junction of Blackburn Road is a triangular shaped Island which contains a telephone booth, a bus shelter, and a couple of fir trees. A highlight of the Christmas Season is the switch on of the Christmas lights on the trees.

Many people attend and are involved in this very happy ceremony including the three councillors for the ward who are at the moment Councillors John Walsh, Hilary Fairclough and Paul Wild. In 2012 the celebration was held on Sunday 2nd December

NATIVITY PAINTINGS

Paul Wild tells us that over 1,000 people turned up to join in the fun. We had carol singing from Sharples Primary, High Lawn Primary, Holy Infants and St Anthony's Primary, St Paul's Primary, Bank Top Brownies and Rainbow Group, and also Sharples Secondary School who also brought along their samba band and school orchestra. There was mulled wine, mince pies, tangerines, and sweets for the children all free but any donations were gratefully accepted and £300 was raised in donations on the day which will be shared amongst the local charities and organisations who helped. Team Eagley Bank and St Paul's Church Community Group who provided stalls and helped organise the event. The highlight of the afternoon were the nativity paintings on display which had been produced by

Sharples Primary, High Lawn Primary, St Paul's Primary,Holy Infants and St Anthony's Primary, and Sharples Secondary School.

As we enter Andrew Lane on our left is an attractive piece of parkland, which has been landscaped over a council tip.

To our right in the 1930s were meadows stretching to Bank top Village. These fields are now covered with private houses, and also a school. The old gated driveway to Sharples Hall from Andrew Lane is now Sharples Hall Drive, a proper road serving the great housing development this locality has seen over the past 50 or 60 years. On our right is The Oaks Primary School opened in 1974. The school has just over 200 pupils.

If we go back to the 1940s the view from Sharples Hall was very different than today. Looking south east we would with the exception of a few houses on Ashworth Lane would see acres of green meadows through to Crompton Way.

Since the war 3 new schools and hundreds of houses have been built.

SHARPLES OR OLLERTON HALL

SHARPLES HALL

Sharples Hall is on our left. It was called Ollerton Hall before the original Sharples Hall was demolished on the building of Sir John Holden's Mill in the 1920s The Lawson's became owners until John Sharple Lawson died in1816; this is how the Lawsons Arms, now the Three Pigeons got its name.

The 1881 census is the first to record Ollerton Hall. It was then the home of John Ashworth who employed 250 workers in his cotton mill. He was born at The Oaks in 1826. John died in 1888 At Ollerton
In the 19th September 1919 issue of the Bolton Journal and Guardian, an article together with a photograph as it then appeared, tells us that a James Rothwell had acquired the hall in1749. It does beg the question "was the house already built when James Rothwell made the purchase, or was it possibly partly built?" The article goes on to say that over the main entrance was an inscription RRR 1749 (Richard Rainshaw Rothwell), and also the arms of the Marquis de Rothwell.

It is assumed that when this place was built they brought the stones from some other residence since the building described and illustrated was a 19th century house. Another mystery is why does the inscription have the letters RRR? as Richard Rainshaw Rothwell wasn't born here until 27th January 1771. Is it possible that the inscription was made well after the house was bought by James Rothwell.

James was vicar of Deane in 1712, he bought the avowson or patronage of Sephton. He had a son Richard who became the Rector of Sephton on 12th January 1763. His father James is listed as patron. Richard served Sephton until his death on 18th September 1801. Some eight months past before the Bishop asked Richard to succeed his father as Rector. He became Rector 3rd May 1802 and was Rector for 62 years. He died on Easter Sunday 5th April 1863 aged 92. He was a bachelor and very popular. People came from other neighbourhoods and villages to hear him preach.

As Rector of Sephton Parish church his living was £30/ 1/ 8 per annum (History Directory & Gazetteer of the County Palatine of Lancashire). He was quite a sportsman especially at swimming and boxing. Also for many, many years he cut half an acre of grass regularly. In his latter years he became quite miserly but still died a very wealthy man. He was buried on19th March1890 in Sephton and his home was shown as Sharples Hall although as I have already said the 1881 census names the hall as Ollerton. He bought land in London and named one street Rothwell Street and another he named Sharples Hall Street. Ramsey Street in Astley Bridge was originally Rothwell Street, and across Blackburn Road opposite, is Rainshaw Street.
His name is engraved on bells 3&4 in Liverpool Cathedral.

CLOCK TOWER AT REAR OF HALL

OLLERTON

One interesting problem researching Ollerton's history is where did the name Ollerton come from? There does not seem to be any obvious reason for the choice, such as a family name, a place like village or town where a person or family originated. There was a related branch of the Lancashire Rothwells living in Lincolnshire. Thomas Willoughby 1st Baron Middleton married Elizabeth Rothwell on 9th April 1736 their main residence was Wollaton Hall. At last, I thought I had a possible connection with the name Wollaton and Ollerton, but unfortunately . although the two names sound a little similar, it was a red herring.

During my research into where the house name "Ollerton" came from I found that prior to the Bretherton's taking residence, people in the past were shown as living at Sharples with little mention of the Hall. Was it convenient to call it the hall with it being a "grand building" and the wealthy ignoring the fact that there was already a Sharples Hall? If it had adopted the name, my feeling is that the Bretherton's made the change and is possibly a corruption of one or two words or names.

On 15th October 1805 Joseph Bretherton married Martha Ellen Appleton at St. Nicholas, Liverpool. They went to live at the hall. They had two children. James, born about 1806, and Ann 1807.

In 1824 an indenture shows that Mr Joseph Bretherton who died in 1810 and whose residence is shown as Sharples, left a will leaving everything to Ellen his wife, there is no mention of the children; however executors are shown as Bartholomew Bretherton, the deceased brother, Richard Leonard, the deceased brother in law, and Ellen, Josephs widow. We know that Ellen, Richard Leonard and his wife Ann were living in the hall in 1824. My thoughts are that Ellen and Joseph probably named the house after their respective names. The word Ollerton contains the three letters from the middle of Ellen's name LLE and the last four letters from Joseph's family name RTON. As most couples refer to their house as ours, is this where the O comes from, giving us the word OLLERTON. Maybe this romantic slant on the house name is the answer, as it would not be the first time a corruption of man and wife names have been arranged to name their house. Whilst this sounds quite romantic there is more. John Holden and his wife to be went carol singing at Ollerton Hall, and he promised Emma Caswell that if she would marry him he would buy the hall. Needless to say she married him and true to his promise he bought Ollerton Hall in 1920.

George, Sir John's eldest son moved into Ollerton, and his youngest son moved into Hill Cot

Just prior to Sir John Holden buying the hall the Journal and Guardian reported that the hall had been acquired as a nursing home for 14 patients.

There is on record another Richard Rainshaw Rothwell born at Sharples Hall in 1809 who was a lawyer, landowner and philanthropist who was created Count de Rothwell by Charles the 2nd,Prince of Monaco. Where this RRR came from is a mystery as I cannot find details of his parents or history. Unfortunately with there being so many Richards in the Rothwell family, and also two houses carrying the name of Sharples Hall, research is very confusing. And whilst I have spent quite a lot of time in trying to sort out all the information which I had, I could well have made mistakes with my research and stand to be corrected. Also although I have no proof I feel that Rothwell family were the first to call the building Sharples Hall.
Sharples Hall Drive becomes Thornham Drive.

Returning to Andrew Lane we come to another older populated part of the village. This is an area of stone cottages which are in the Eagley Bank Conservation area. (In the row of cottages was the Co-op which was one of the five B.C.S stores in the Astley Bridge). Many of the stone building in the Astley Bridge part of the conservation area are listed buildings. Park Row, Playfair Street Park Terrace, Ollerton Terrace, Makant's Farm, Sandbanks. Etc. whilst it may sound good living in a conservation area it has its drawbacks as there are certain rules and regulations to be adhered too. The Eagley Conservation Area affects not only parts of Astley Bridge but also Eagley itself.

PARK VIEW

There was a children's park facing Park View, unfortunately it
has gone the way of other recreation areas, making way for
house building. Andrew Lane finally ends with Eagley Brow
meets Eagley Way, which was opened in May 1948. Bollards
were placed at the exit of Andrew Lane, thus stopping the Lane
being used to get to Eagley.

As we come to Eagley Bridge and the old bus terminus this is
the end of the old route of the road to Blackburn through Astley
Bridge.

Eagley mills were built in 1796 by John Wakefield. James
Chadwick and his brother Robert bought the mills .in 1820.
They amalgamated with J N Phillips of Manchester in 1830. The
Phillips family wanted a better standard of living for their
workers hence the start of building the model village.

EAGLEY BROOK, ON THE LEFT ASTLEY BRIDGE ON THE RIGHT EAGLEY

There is quite an active community group in the area known as Team Eagley Bank, who do sterling work raising money for various charities, in fact just recently Hilary Fairclough, the local councillor held a coffee morning at her home which raised £200 for the Trussel Trust an organisation helping the poor. The team have also been engaged in litter picking together with Paul and Hilary helping to keep the area tidy. The team are a band of dedicated local residents helping to make the world a better place for all. I feel sure that Councillor John Walsh has been involved with "The Team" probably with the Christmas lights.

SEYMOUR ROAD

Seymour Road about 200 years or so ago was just a farm track leading to Old Nell's Farm and New House Farm, even Sharples Farm was not built until 1843, although there could have been a farm on the site before.

Seymour Road together with Sharples Park was at one time the Chorley New Road of the village, with many large houses, as well as equally large gardens. In fact by today's standards at least six of their owners, if not more would have been classed as multi- millionaires. These thorough-fares became favourites for the more wealthy and middle class people of the town.
Some years ago the council decided to close the entrance to Seymour Road with the intention of stopping the road becoming short cut from Crompton Way to Blackburn Road, and visa versa. Great circular blocks were put onto the carriageway at the Crompton Way end of the road. The idea initially seemed to be good to people outside the area, however it created a lot of controversy especially for the people who lived in the area and used the road regularly. Detours of around a mile were necessary for the residents living on or around Seymour Road. The barriers have now gone and the road is a through road again.

On the corner of Blackburn Road and Seymour Road was a chemist shop owned by Maurice John Hall, which eventually was taken over and belonged for many years by Knott Bros Chemists, and Pharmacists, Photographer Supplies. They were also family grocers and Italian Warehousemen. At a later date a post office was added.
So as a business they covered a wide variety of household needs. Their first shop was No1 Blackburn Road, facing what was then Kay Street. This shop was run by P Knott whilst the Seymour Road shop was run by H Knott.

Eventually the Bolton Co-operative Society took over the business, but I think the post office part went its separate way and become a business in its own right on the other side of Blackburn Road. The Co-op closed down selling the premises to Walsh's who were, "Protective Clothing Manufacturers".

KNOTT BROS MANAGED BY HERBERT KNOTT

Alongside these premises on Seymour Road are a number of stone cottages, followed by Palm Street. Originally this was Holland Street, until I think, 1928 when Crompton Way opened. The new Road cut the top half of Holland Street in to two. The Palm Street portion never really had a direct link with the rest of the street except over what in the early 1900s was a piece of spare land just west of Beech Hill house and gardens.
The Beeches at a later date became South View.

THE THEATRE CHURCH

On the other side of the road are the Theatre Church buildings.
Methodism started in Bolton when the first service was held in
the Old Nags Head Yard on 1st November 1747. The Society
was formed in Bolton by John Bennet one of John Wesley's
nine assistants. John Wesley came to Bolton on 28th August
1748, and again 18th October 1749.

John Bennet was a very good evangelist and through a lot of his
endeavours Methodism was established in a powerful way in the
northwest. However there were disagreements between him and
John Wesley, especially over a young lady called Grace Murray.
The two men did not see eye to eye on some doctrines, and also
William Bennet married Grace Murray on 3rd October 1749 in
the prescience of Rev John Whitefield and Rev Charles Wesley.
Although, it was thought at the time she was engaged to John
Wesley. Needless to say John Bennet left the Methodist
movement. John Bennet became the minister at Dukes Alley
Chapel a nonconformist church which was at the start of
Congregationalism not only in Bolton but the rest of the
country.

The first Methodist meetings were held in Long Row, now Whitehill Cottages off Belmont Road, and there were some difficulties as the meetings moved from house to house. For a number of years they met in Mr and Mrs Woods house in Kelly Row. When the Anglicans moved from Ash Grove to their new church St Pauls in 1848 the Methodists moved in and with help of Bridge Street Methodists bought Ash Grove in 1853 for £200. The Sunday school grew rapidly from 96 scholars in 1853 to 332 scholars, and 31 officers and teachers. In 1864 they sold the building for £240. In 1865 preliminary steps were taken to build a new chapel. Land was leased from the Earl of Wilton in Seymour Road and the Cornerstone of the new chapel was laid on7th September 1866, total cost £5,000, and the first service in the new chapel was held on 22nd April 1868.

By 1871a new day school was opened on 9th January, followed by an infant's school in 1882. In 1893 further extensions were made to both chapel and school.

I can recall that during the war we were taken from St Pauls School to watch Ministry of Information Films in the school yard. The films were shown on a small screen, about six feet wide by four feet high. Which was mounted on a soft top truck which was about the size of the old Morris Minor. As the screen was well shaded being well back inside the vehicle. As children, we enjoyed the novelty of not only watching the film but also getting half a day away from school. The only drawback was, that as usually happens when as school children we do something out of the ordinary instead of class work, we have to write an essay on the experience.

Sadly in 1954 the day school closed, and by 1964 with falling numbers it was felt right to demolish and reconstruct the buildings to accommodate 250-300 people.

1 To demolish the building and reconstruct the church
2 To halve the existing building
3 To demolish the existing building and extend the lecture hall.

In 1966 Rev Leslie Marsh arrived and suggested converting the church building into a Theatre Church. The church sold its cricket field at High View to the council and the money raised would help to finance the alterations. The Theatre Church opened on 19th July 1969.

As a theatre, its first production was a musical "Joan" written by the Rev Marsh with over 1,400 people going to see the show. The same year, the Sunday school buildings were converted into a conference centre. In 1985 the centre was extended.

Again sadly, the Theatre Church has close and been sold, a big effort by local operatic and drama organisations got together and started a fund to try to buy the buildings but to no avail.

Many organisations used the building beside the musical and drama companies. The Church is a very handsome building *being built of red brick highlighted with stone; it really* is a gem and like Astley Bridge Library part of the villages heritage. Here again, another nail has been put in Astley Bridges community coffin.

The Bolton News reported on 10th September that the The Crystal Theatre, Function and Wedding Halls organisation had bought the complex for around £500,000. When Amateur dramatic groups enquired about hiring the hall they were given a charge of £70,000 per year to rent the complex except for the halls of residence. Needless to say the rent was a great increase on what the groups had paid earlier, and really was a non starter.

Behind the church are a cluster of terraced streets such as Norton and Gresham Streets, beyond there are some allotments then Astley Brook.

At numbers 36 and 38 Seymour Road was the George Gould Williams Commercial and Boarding School. Whilst the term boarding is used the census of both 1891 and 1901, the census does not record any students living there. G. G. Williams was born in Ipswich. It was still a school in 1932 and Mr Adam Bruce was principle.

By coincidence at number 40 lived the Rev George Williams.

At number 62 Thomas Holmes and family lived before moving to Hayward Leigh in Sharples Park.

Number 45 is now Seymour Road (privately owned) Nursery. Next door is Dormer Street, originally called Holly Place. This is where the Gospel Hall in Maxwell Street first held their meetings in the home of Mr and Mrs Martin. During the last war the Auxiliary Fire Service had a Fire Station on Dormer Street. On the other side of the road stood number 49 which was Linwood House home of G Hesketh and family of T M Hesketh and Sons.

At number 51 was Strathmore where a Mr Sydney Newton lived. Prior to him was a John Livy a surgeon. Strathmore is now a nursing home.

At number 53 lived Alexander Duxbury, a paper manufacturer at Hall i'th Wood Paper mill
His brother Roger also a partner in the business lived at number 64.

THE DUXBURY FAMILY

Yates Duxbury was born 9th February 1818 he was the first of Andrews 13 children
His father was Andrew Duxbury a cotton firm bookkeeper.
His grandfather was a lay preacher, and spent most of his time preaching the gospel rather than making a fortune.
At the tender age of 7 Yates was sent to learn the art of paper making. His schooling was limited to 3 to 4 years, in fact he was essentially self taught. When he married his wife Hannah Kay, he signed the marriage certificate but Hannah could only make her mark.

Yates worked in the paper industry slowly climbing the ladder, he moved around various companies as foreman, and manager, he had plenty of ups and downs, then in 1863 he secured the business of Thomas Crook for £1,200. They made calendar bowl paper at Hall I'th Wood paper mill.

Cotton, linen, wool fibres are used exclusively in various combinations for different grades of paper. Elasticity, colour uniformity, and durability are important qualities needed for this type of paper. It is used for gloss finish in magazines etc.

He put his son Andrew in charge. Yates was a strict orthodox Wesleyan going to bed sharp at 8-30 pm, and rising at 5-45 am. Andrew and his father worked happily together for some ten years, and then things started to deteriorate between the two. Before he joined his father he was manger of a paper mill but with his father he was under manager.

Andrew always wanted his own mill, and then the opportunity came for him to purchase an unused mill. Heap Bridge Paper Mill. Then in 1882 Andrew must have written to his father and Yates decided to help with the money. Unfortunately within two years Andrew went bankrupt, and within twelve months died at 47 years of age a broken and disheartened man.

Yates had five other sons, Alexander, Roger, and Yates Jnr, followed their father into the business. All three had served their apprenticeship with other companies. They joined their father at Hall I'th Wood. A year after Andrews's death Yates bought the Heap Bridge Mill paying off the debt. He delegated Roger to run it.

Yates live in the Cottage by the Hall I'th Wood mill and died in 1888 aged 73

At number 59 "Wilton Grange" lived the William Inglis family.

William was born in Ottawa, Canada. He started work as an apprentice in 1852 at the St Lawrence Engine works in Montreal. In 1856 he came to Britain and worked at the

Glasgow firm of R Napier and Sons. During his time there he attended engineering classes at Glasgow University. In 1858 He moved on to work at Robert Stephenson and C, returning to Canada in 1860 where he was engaged in designing and erecting machinery. He supervised the building of the hull of the paddle steamer "Montreal". In 1867 he was appointed engineering manager of Hick Hargreaves, at Soho Iron Works. Eventually he became a partner. William was a brilliant engineer, he had a quiet and self possessed manner, was kind and considerate to those over whom he had authority. Sadly he died at his home, "Wilton Grange" in the prime of his working life on April 22nd 1890, from pneumonia after only a few days of illness.

Making our way towards Crompton Way we pass a number of roads, the oldest of which is probably Dormer Street. This is where the Gospel Hall in Maxwell Street first held their meetings in the home of Mr and Mrs Martin.
During the last war the Auxiliary Fire Service had a Fire Station on Dormer Street.

ACDOCO

Further down Seymour Road we come to Mallinson Street, home of Acdo. The company was started in the kitchen of Harry Pilling and his mother's home. They produced the product and named it Acdo, then cut it into blocks similar to washing soap, and it wrapped ready for sale.
When the housewives used it, it had to be grated into the wash. I believe, that if you saved three wrappers the company would give you a free grater in exchange, again I believe that Harry worked on the principle on his selling price, a third producing, a third promoting etc. and a third profit. I can recall Acdo demonstrations when I was a young boy. Harry would use church halls and other community establishments for washing

exhibitions and to promote sales. Harry also used another incentive to promote sales at the venues, and that he would organise a free draw for a ten shilling note.

I can remember Acdo being exhibited at the Bolton Co-operative Society central shop in Bridge Street. I understand that working conditions were good and good and fair wages were paid to his employees.

Even though there was great pressure on the business from the big boys, i.e. Unilever and Proctor and Gamble. Acdo managed to hold its own. Not only that, the Acdo brand was exported to many parts of the world. I personally have seen Acdo products on the shelves in Spain.

I recall another product, that was Clebo, but unfortunately it did not do too well and was discontinued. However, undaunted Marshal, Harry's son became Managing Director and another product was introduced which became a hit and winner, that was Glo-White which eventually became 50%of the business. Time has moved on since Mum and Harry started in their kitchen and there are many more products in the Acdoco range.

After passing a number of semi detached houses, Orchard Avenue, Ventnor Avenue, and Carisbrook Drive we come to the Seymour Road entrance to Crompton Way. A few years ago Bolton Council in their wisdom decided to close Seymour Road at this junction, I believe that this was done to stop people taking a short cut from Crompton Way to Blackburn Road and vice versa. However the locals objected because they could have to make a detour of up to a mile to and from Crompton Way. Eventually the Council relented and the road blocks have been removed.

Just to the right after Carisbrook Drive was a derelict cobbled cart track, this is now just an asphalted footpath. Bollards have been erected to stop its use by vehicles. Originally the track gave access to Bank House which was the Thwaites family home before Watermillock was built, to Hall House Farm.

Beyond the farm were some water filter beds. The cobbled track would be a well used by many of the workers in Eden and Thwaites Waters Meeting Bleach works which was built in 1863. The track met up with a footpath leading down some steps from Crompton Way. I believe that these steps were a short cut aid for people going to work at the bleachworks. James H Longworth in his book "The Cotton Mills of Bolton 1780-1985" tells us (slightly paraphrased)Eden and Thwaites joined together as a bleachers partnership in 1836, taking over the Sharples Bleachworks built and run by Nightingale and Southworth in 1821-1822. In 1836 they sold it to the Murton family and there is some doubt when the works closed down. It was probably in the early 1900s. By 1853 James Eden and Thomas Thwaite had built another bleachworks at Waters Meeting which was operating until 1925 when Hay and Smith joined the partnership. The bleachworks closed in 1962.
The Evening News dated 13th June 1873 reported (paraphrased) that Mr Robert Knott a manager at Eden and Thwaites Bleachworks Waters Meeting had invented a plan whereby sewage of the whole of the town and district may be utilised, and at half the cost of Burnden Sewage works. The experiments would be carried out in a field just off Blackburn Road, there is no detail of the site, however I feel that the area is probably on the north side of Astley Brooke below Norton Street to Mallinson Street. Most of the area is now covered with trees but I remember over 50 years ago it being flat and clear with some kind of workings which could easily have been settling tanks and pits for Mr Knott's experiments.
A mixture which he invented would be dropped into the tanks, and he guarantees that in less than 24 hours the filthiest water from any sewer will be transformed into the purest crystal water of which the most fastidious of taste would not refuse to drink. The cost he claims will be half of the Burnden Works which he understands is £20 per week.

On the corner of Seymour Road and Crompton way was a small wooded area which was cleared some time after the last war on which two bungalows have been built.

About two to three hundred yards from south east was a Boggart Hole. A Bogart is a mischievous poltergeist, and is up to no good. He makes things disappear, turns milk sour, moves things around and altogether is a rather unpleasant soul.

WATERMILLOCK & GATEHOUSE

1887

ENGLISH HERITAGE IMAGES

The Watermillock together with its gatehouse are two of the gems of Astley Bridge buildings which are still standing. As heritage buildings go there are only a few left. Sharples Hall (Ollerton), the Lees, Thornleigh, although this has been altered and extended to make a fine college, Astley Bridge Library Building, and next door the Public Office Building. Sir John Holden's Mill. Hill Cot, now part of Sharples Secondary school. Others that have been demolished are, High Lawn, the Thorns, the Beeches, Whitehill (Wilkinsons), Eden's Orphanage, Yew Tree House, and Thornydykes.

Thomas Thwaites was the person responsible for the building of the Watermillock Mansion. He lived nearby in Bank House, and the architects for the Watermillock were Messrs Bradshaw and Gass. The building was started in 1880 and finished in 1882, unfortunately Thomas died before the house was finished and his son took over.

Thomas's choice of site was excellent and inspired as the building stood on a rise overlooking Eagley Brook to the East with the nearest house being Hall I'th Wood. Beyond the hall was the railway track..

On the west the nearest houses in those days were in Holland Street with the exception of Old Nell's, and New House farms, and just north of them was Lower House. Behind the mansion was a great expanse of meadows right up to Sharples Hall farm. In those days the Watermillock would dominate the skyline and would be seen for miles around.

The entrance to the house was from Seymour Road, as Crompton Way wasn't built until 1928. In fact, the building of Crompton Way sliced a great chunk of land from the estate. Originally there was quite a long drive from the gatehouse, or if you prefer the porters lodge, which in itself a very attractive building, and the gateway to the mansion through tree lined, landscaped gardens and lawns.

As I have already said, Thomas Thwaites died before the house was finished, and on the day of his funeral flags flew at half mast on all the mills and bleachworks, and all shops and houses closed their blinds, as Thomas was a very well respected man in the village.

Children from Eden's orphanage and GG Williams's boarding school lined the pavement near St Paul's church.

The hearse was drawn by four black horses. In the procession walked 32 of his workpeople accompanied by numerous carriages and coaches. Thomas was laid to rest in Walmsley church graveyard. Probably by this time St Paul's graveyard was full. Thomas's son, Herbert took over the job of seeing Watermillock mansion being completed. Herbert owned what may have been the first Daimler in Bolton.

Not only was Watermillock a handsome house from the outside, but there was no expense spared with the furnishings inside. The materials used were only of the top quality, panelled walls, beautiful fireplaces and décor. There were many rooms in the building including billiard, and smoke rooms, and also ample cellar rooms. There was a large coach house and stables. What you would call a real Gentleman's House.

Herbert did not stay at Watermillock for long and I understand that his wife did not stay there at all. When he moved out a Mr Joseph Marsden took it on a short lease. He retired to Worthing. Before the First World War a doctor Schofield bought the house and was used as a military hospital during the war. Later it became an Anglican Retreat for the Manchester Diocese.

Colonel Hesketh of Hill Fold Mills owned it for a time. He used to let the scouts camp in the grounds of the house.

The building was purchased by the Rev H.B. Morse who had planned to use the stone for a new church building for St Aidans near the railway track at Tonge Moor; however the project never got off the ground. The Journal and Guardian of 11th June 1937 reported that 50 Basque children had arrived at the Watermillock very tired. The children came from San Sebastian in Spain. They had seen fighting and had endured bombing raids. The children travelled up from Southampton on two busses which were pulled up by the police for speeding but under the circumstances the police took no action. Other accounts say that there were 38 refugees.

Porridge was on the menu at breakfast, this was something that the children hadn't eaten before, but the must have enjoyed it as just like Oliver Twist they asked for more.

Eventually the house was used for a Nursing |Home. It became empty for a while and in 1994 it was bought by Wolverhampton and Dudley Breweries who converted it into a restaurant and bar. In 1999 Decker's Restaurants bought the brewery and refurbished the building at a cost of about half a million pounds. There have been many ghostly sightings in the building, staff refuse to go down to the cellars on their own, complaining of a male presence which looks out from one of the rooms, many have said that he wears a top hat and a long cloak.

On the 28th February 2012 a team of investigators stayed at the Watermillock to check if the house was haunted. The report on the internet by Joanne tells us of their findings. In one room, one of the groups sensed an old man whilst another stated to smell a dirty, trampy, cheesy foot smell, and a drop in temperature.

In another room one of the team felt the touch of what felt like an ice cube on the back of the hand, then the presence of a man who was big and muscular. There were many other encounters during the evening in various parts of the building and the conclusion arrived at by the team was that the Watermillock was haunted. Various groups of ghost hunters spend an evening in the house for a ghostly experience.

To the east of the building is a road. Between the road and Watermillock was a cricket field belonging to All Souls Church in Astley Street. The field hasn't been used for cricket for quite a good number of years, but looking at the site now via Google Earth, from the few markings on the pitch it looks as though it has been used pretty recently for football or rugby. The road goes down past the old cricket field to what was originally Hall I'th Wood Paper mill, this has long since gone. Over the years the buildings have been used by many companies, and are now occupied by Bentelers who are a worldwide company employing 29,400 people at 170 locations in 38 countries. In 1876 Carl Benteler started the business by opening an ironmongers shop in Bielefield, Germany. Over time the business grew by building engineering works which produced steel tubes and other products. They also expanded by the acquisition of other companies. One interesting fact is that the Benteler Global Procurement GmbH is located in Paderborn a twin town with Bolton.

Since Crompton Way was built in 1928, many houses have been erected on the road towards Blackburn Road. In the fifties old peoples bungalows were built in Watermillock Gardens. Many semi- detached buildings were built in Sunnymeade Avenue, Weythorne Drive, and Almond Street all these streets etc leading off Crompton Way. Facing Almond Street is a post war private estate development which leads from and includes Stambourne Drive.

Before Crompton Way was built there was a country lane which ran from Berry Fold, off what became School Street, now Newnham Street, past Old Nell's Farm, behind St Paul's Church through to Lower House, just below Florence Avenue Allotments. This lane had the quaint name of Old Wash.

The building of Crompton Way cut the lane in two. The entrance to northern part of the lane in the 1930s and 40s was an ideal spot for the police in their Wolsley cars to lie in wait for a passing unsuspecting motorist speeding down Crompton Way. If the police thought the driver was breaking the speed limit, they would pull out and chase the culprit with their bell ringing to warn the motorist to stop. In those days police cars were not equipped with sirens.

As we proceeded down the lane we pass New House Farm, before coming to a five barred gate some 100 yards before we cross a footpath which leads from Rainshaw Street to West Glen

This footpath is bordered on either side with hen pens and allotments, and there is a subterranean stream running alongside the path. A friend of our family owned a market garden alongside this footpath, and his only water supply was what he could collect from the roofs of his buildings, so he decided to dig a well. He dug down about four feet very close to the footpath and suddenly the bottom of the hole filled with water. Needless to say he was more than pleased with his luck, and he was showing my dad the well, my dad knowing of this underground stream told his friend Harold that he had tapped into the stream but Harold was not convinced. There is one thing for sure Harold was never again short of water.

As we cross the footpath we pass Lower House, which at one time could have been a farm although even checking old maps I have no proof of this. The lane finishes at the end of Florence Avenue having past the southern entrance to Florence Avenue allotments.

WEST GLEN

West Glen or Mason Clough commonly known locally as the
W.G. was a lovely valley, with a bubbling stream called with the
delightful name of Barley Brook running through. The brook
probably started life as a field drain around where Oaks school
stands, and by the time the water had reached Ashworth Lane it
had grown into a sparkling stream. The brook runs from
Ashworth Lane, through a heavily wooded valley with some
very steep sides for some 300 yards or more, and then it goes
through a small picturesque horse shoe shaped tunnel for about
20 yards.
There was a footstone bridge crossing the stream some thirty
yards from the tunnel. The bridge was made from three great
slabs of stone some eight or so feet long by about two feet wide
and roughly nine inches deep which, over the past 60 years have
broken up and there is little evidence of a stone bridge ever
being there. How and where these great stone came from is a

mystery as the approach from any direction is very limited. The brook then bubbles its way through the heart of what was a beautiful quite open valley, then for some reason, probably, when the footpath was being constructed, a pipe was laid to stop erosion of the banking and the destruction of the foot path. This *is exactly what happened further downstream. On its journey it* passed through the pipe for about 15 to 20 yards.

The pipe was roughly two feet in diameter and over the years has become blocked, and the stream has made its own way to meet up with Eagley Brook about 400 yards from the end of the glen.

As I have said West Glen was a lovely spot in the 1920s, 30s, and 40s. It pictured on a number of post cards as a place to visit, and picnic. Whilst it was no where as popular as Barrow Bridge *it was one of the treasures of Astley Bridge. I feel sure that the* footpaths leading to, and through the glen are ancient rights of way.

As the footpath made its way out of the valley towards Bank Top it continued between two flourishing hedgerow fences dividing two what were lovely meadows. About half way along the path were two five barred gates one on either side of the footpath which allowed the farmer access from one meadow to the other. Both these fields have been built on since the last war and are now part of the Whitegate private housing estate. As a result the path has been rerouted behind the estate.

I believe, although I have no proof that the footpaths through the valley were at one time maintained by the Ashworth's of New Eagley Mills for the benefit of their workers walking from the south of what is now Crompton Way via, and passing New house Farm, with the people from higher up Blackburn Road using the footpath from Rainshaw Street.

As a child I have spent many hours each week in the valley, playing in the brook, walking through the tunnel with my head nearly between my knees because the tunnel was so small and low, climbing the trees, making swings with a piece of rope attached to a strong branch. Sadly as years went by the footpaths were neglected and started to disintegrate. Mother Nature has now taken charge and the valley is now overgrown and has lost its beauty and tranquillity.

On each side of the valley from the tunnel to Ashworth Lane were many hen pens, and smallholdings, the footpaths to these were not very safe due to the sheer drop to the valley floor. Alas these were not maintained in any way and the pen holders had to make their way very carefully to their plots.

On our way back to Crompton Way, we come through another post war development which swallowed up Astley Bridge football ground, and New House farm and land, with further housing development where Hill Davidson's "Holly Mills" Towel Mill stood.

On the south side of Crompton Way, Old Wash became Almond Street, it was a street of two halves. From Newnham Street (originally School Street) to Nell Street was paved, but from Nell Street to Crompton Way was unadopted and a cinder and dirt track with the part of the carriageway being a lot lower than what we would consider the pavement. However some time after the war the street was adopted and paved.

Semi- detached houses were on one side of the undeveloped street, and on the other side was John Ashworth's New Mill (Holland Street)

On the Almond Street, Crompton Way corner stands The Crompton Chapel of the Co-operative Funeral Services Ltd. Prior to the chapel stood the pavilion firstly, of Astley Bridge Cricket Club until it moved to Sharples Park, then some time later it was taken over as changing rooms for Astley Bridge Football Club, who developed what was left of the cricket ground after it being cut down in size by the building of Crompton Way into a compact football pitch surrounded with a reasonable amount of standing room for supporters. On the main road side was a covered stand which was well used in inclement weather. I suppose that it was one of the few grounds were teams changed into their kit then had to cross a main road to play football. The ground maintenance equipment was also stored in the changing rooms.

There were two entrances to the ground one was a double gated opposite the changing rooms, whilst the other was a small entrance at the Blackburn Road end of the ground. This way into the ground had a small box office type hut. I understand the entrance fee before the war was 3d, but after the war it was 6d. A big problem for the club was that it only had good fences on two sides.

The original football club was known as Astley Bridge Wanderers but it became defunct sometime around 1900 when I believe the ground was used for the building of houses. I am not sure but believe that the club using the Crompton way ground had anything to do with the Wanderers as there is a 30 year gap between the two clubs. The new club would have taken over the ground sometime after the opening of Crompton Way in 1928 and probably in its early days played friendly games with local teams. In those days there was no shortage of teams from pub teams, Bolton district teams to "A" teams of the football League.

The latter club entered the West Lancashire league some time in the early 1930s. In 1936 they finished 9th. The League closed

down for the duration of the war restarting in 1945/6, but sadly the team was relegated joining the Lancashire Combination.
On its north side was Hill, Davidson Ltd. Holly Mills who were towel manufacturers. The mill was opened in 1925 and many of their customers were coal mine operators, with the towels being used in the pit head baths. Their products were of the highest quality with an excellent terry giving good drying qualities and also a hard wearing product. Mr Davidson, I believe, was the main salesman and there is a story of him going to see a buyer in a national company which had shops up and down the country. The buyer had a rule that only one case of samples could be brought in at any time, but Mr Davidson wanted to show him all the samples of the two cases he had with him. He took one case in opened it, and immediately said to the buyer "I'm sorry I have brought the wrong case in" before the buyer could say anything he left the case with the buyer and rushed out to bring in the second case. I don't know if Mr Davidson got an order but he did manage to beat the buyers rule.

During the war they, like many other companies had to close by order of the government, in fact between one third and a half of manufacturing firms were closed for the duration of the war. However the companies which were allowed to stay open had to supply goods to the companies closed. The reason being, that although your company as a manufacturing unit it could still supply its own customers. This was to stop the working factories from poaching people away from their normal suppliers, and also lack of demand and man power due to wartime conditions. I do not know when this regulation came into force; it must have been a little while after the war started as the company built a large air raid shelter in the grounds. Alas, there was little need for it during the day as the company ran on a skeleton staff of two men plus management. The skeleton staff and management undertook the jobs of parcelling towels ready for shipment, maintaining the building, heating the building especially in winter to help stop any deteriation of equipment.

The management of Holly Mills kindly let the local people use the shelter during the night.

When the war ended and regulations were relaxed, Mr Hill and Mr Davidson wasted little time at all in reopening the mill. They contacted as many of their pre war weavers, warpers and ancillary workers, to get the factory going. In practically in no time the mill was again producing towels. The air raid shelter was quickly refurbished as a canteen.

In 1985 the mill was bought by the big cotton conglomerate Dorma. Sadly a few years later it closed and was demolished. Prior to the mill being built there were many hen pens and allotments on some of the land.

The dividing fence between the mill and football ground was only three feet high with just three cross members, making it very easy to squash through, or climb over. The main deterrent from trying to sneak into the ground from this side was the perimeter wall surrounding the other three sides of the mill, although there was a narrow footpath from Rainshaw Street allotments through some allotments and hen pens to the mill yard.

On the west side of the ground the first thirty yards or so was protected by advertising hoarding but the rest of the boundary was wide open. Although to get to this boundary, people had to go through land owned by Norman Lomax who had a garage on Crompton Way. The club was never overrun with spectators, probably averaging 150 per home game.

During the last war the club closed for the duration, and whilst the pitch deteriorated and weeds started to take over, in fact where the centre circle was there was a mass of quite tall thistles. Many local children myself included, used the ground as a park. During the war both St Paul's and Seymour Road Methodist schools were allocated a piece of land on the north side terraces for the production of vegetables. Incidentally the terraces were not paved except under the stand.

Soon after the war ended, the club restarted, and after a lot of work getting the ground back into reasonable condition football came back to Astley Bridge. To help boost funds when the season had ended the club staged knock out medal competitions. These proved very popular with many local teams taking part. There would be three to four hundred spectators attending especially when the competitions got near to the final. It wasn't unusual to see many of the Bolton Wanderers players of the day like Nat Lofthouse, Willie Moir, Stan Hanson, and others regularly coming to watch the matches. By the mid 60s interest started to wane and the club finished. The ground was sold for housing.

Back to Crompton Chapel. Mrs Anne Davenport, whose husband Albert eventually was appointed manager said that The Co-operative Funeral Service started in 1937 in Ulleswater Street. The Co-op bought a house and garage in Ulleswater Street from Fred Snaylam and Sons, a well known local haulage contractor.

Later a small office was established in the men's tailoring department in Bark Street. A Chapel of Repose was opened and dedicated on 22nd may 1948.

In 1971 the department built a new Chapel of Repose for £20,000 on Crompton Way. It stands on the site of the old cricket pavilion, and was dedicated by the Bishop of Manchester Rev Patrick C Roger on29th July 1971.

In 1911, R Clifton Lomax set up in business on Blackburn Road as a general dealer in 1911. As time went by it became known as an ironmongers. In 1922 he opened a motor repair garage in Holland Street (his son Norman inherited the businesses) took over some land which at one time was partly the site of a large Bolton Waterworks service reservoir. He built and opened a garage "Central Garage" on the north side of Crompton Way.

In the olden days there were not many cars on the road, but even so there were many petrol companies each one advertising their own brand of petrol.

Today people get their fuel from a supermarket, or a particular manufacturer's petrol station, such as Shell or Texaco, back then the petrol stations would carry more than one brand of petrol as did the Central Garage, and in those days motorists preferred to keep to the same brand of petrol, the thought was that keeping to the same brand helped the engine to run better.

Clifton Lomax garage in Holland Street was taken over by John Pilkinton for his painting and decorating business.
John Pilkington moved to Moss Bank Way between the park and Manley Terrace.. He built a petrol filling station on the road with premises at the rear for his painting business. The whole site has since been redeveloped.
Jack Poole who once worked for Norman Lomax took over the Holland Street property and opened it, again as a car repair garage,
Central Garage in its time it was quite busy, not only with car repairs but also petrol sales as for some years it was the only petrol station in Astley Bridge.
The land behind the garage wasn't developed except for a few allotments. Just before the last war Norman Lomax built a bank of single garages for rent. These backed on to back Holland Street.
Some time after the end of the war he built another bank of garages facing the others. Even so there was still plenty of derelict land left which was never developed. Norman sold out and the garage changed hands once or twice afterwards until Lidl bought the site, and built their Supermarket and car park..

Moving on into Holland Street, which together with Blackburn Road lost some of its buildings with the building of Crompton Way. In fact the Pack Horse Inn which was only two doors from the Pineapple was pulled down. The number 10 bus service terminus was in Holland Street. Its route took it from Holland Street through Tonge Moor through town and up to Stapleton Avenue.

Later the crossroads on Blackburn Road/ Crompton Way were improve with some road widening. This meant more buildings being demolished including the Grapes Inn, and the Williams Deacons Bank. A proper turn round terminus was built together with a new Williams Deacon Bank.

Before the building of an official terminus the busses used to reverse into Holland Street. Unfortunately on one occasion a bus reversing into Holland Street ran over a Mr Entwistle's foot, who was one of Astley Bridges football club stars playing at outside left.

On the corner of Blackburn Road and Crompton Way stands the Pineapple Inn one of John Hamer's many public houses.

JOHN HAMER

He was Chairman of the Turton district Council in 1941/2, also President of the Bolton Cricket League. The brewery business was started by his grandfather with the purchase of the Volunteer Inn at Bromley Cross in 1853. John had 42 pubs and a brewery which he sold to Dutton's in June 1951 for £316,000. John had a racing stable, and probably his best known horse was Boltonian. John broke his neck in a riding accident in 1934, he recovered fully but he had a series of strokes in 1945. He suffered from depression and eventually he committed suicide 22nd October 1957 whilst living in St Annes.

At the rear of the Pineapple was Frank Crompton's Cycle Shop. About the time the new bus terminus was built Frank Crompton moved to new premises next door but one to the Tramways Hotel. Whether this was a coincidence or by design of the council, but on his leaving the council built new toilets on the cycle shop site. The toilets became quite run down and also were vandalised, and after a period of time being closed they were demolished. I think that the area is now part of the Pineapples Yard.

The Pineapple had a Jug and Bottle entrance on Crompton Way. I recall one of our neighbours walking down to the Pineapple with a large jug nearly every evening for some sustenance. She used the jug and bottle department to save her from the embarrassment of being seen in the pub. In those days it wasn't the done thing for ladies going into a public house on their own. Some years later more improvements were made to the crossroad with destruction of more buildings including the recently built Williams Deacons Bank which was relocated some 200 yards down Blackburn Road.

The number 10 bus route was discontinued, and the terminus, bank building, and two houses on Blackburn Road were demolished as the exit from Crompton way was widened and redeveloped.

In the top half of Holland Street was the old established company of Phillipson's Engineers, and Brush Works. Sadly due to the decline of the cotton industry, business started to wane, and like many companies supplying the needs of the mills made it hard to stay in business.

The premises were taken over by Mechanical Services founded by Mr Barrie Badland. The company is now known as Indespension. The company builds a quite a large range of trailers. As the company grew they moved to larger premises in what was Openshaw's Cotton Mill on Belmont Road. In 2000 The company moved to new premises on Chorley New Road Horwich. Sadly Mr Badland died suddenly in 1982. He was a well respected man, and at Christmas in his first year in Holland Street he gave all the residents nearby the works a lovely hamper.

Still in Holland Street was the company of Isherwood and Fairclough's, a long established company who were wheelwrights. Although there was an entrance and offices in Holland Street their main entrance was on Blackburn Road. An unusual feature of their premises was that their workshop which crossed back Holland Street cutting the back street in two.

The works had a very large sliding gate which was nearly the full width of back street on the south side. This entrance was well used for vehicles going for repair before the 1940s, but with the demise of horse drawn vehicles the back street entrance was not used a great deal after the war. Back Streets on Mondays were no go areas for all vehicles because there were dozens of washing lines crossing the back streets, and woe betide any vehicle wanting to use the back street as its owner would have to face the wrath of the housewives.

The wheelwrights used the ground floor of a house lower down Holland Street. Number 125 as a garage with an entrance from the back street, firstly, for their horse drawn wagon. I am not sure where the horse was stabled, but eventually they used it to garage a motor vehicle. There was a separate entrance from the front of the building to the second floor which the Ladies branch of the Astley Bridge Conservative Party used the upstairs rooms as a meeting place.

The street was named after Sir William de Hollande who was granted the Manor of Sharples by Roger de Sharples in 1315. Holland Street must have been built in phases as there is a mixture of designs and materials used. There are stone cottages at both the top and bottom of the street, with a mixture of red brick buildings in between. The east side of the street was built much later than the west.

106

ASHWORTH'S NEW MILL HOLLAND STREET

JOHN ASHWORTH

John Ashworth a descendant his namesake opened the New Mill
in Holland Street in 1868. Behind the mill on what was once a
gravel pit there was recreation area with a bowling green, and
landscaped gardens where on lovely sunny days the employees
mainly women would sit out enjoying the park like atmosphere.
Bordering on Crompton Way was the mill lodge together with
the inevitable tall mill chimney. On a very cold morning steam
vapour you would see rising from the water.
John Ashworth and family attended St Paul's Church, where
they rented a pew. John paid 2/6 per week to have the pew
carpet shaken.
He also gave one of his labourers a pair of his shoes. The man
resoled them, and gave them a good polish which made them
look like new. The man wore them for work and when John
Ashworth saw them he bought them back for 22/6.
The mill closed in 1960, and was demolished.

SEE BANK TOP FOR MORE INFORMATION OF THE ASHWORTH
FAMILY

Bolton Co-operative Society built a supermarket on the site which opened in 1963. The Co-op put an automatic car wash in the car park. The charge was 20p a wash and I can remember the great queues of cars especially at weekends to take advantage of this great offer. Sadly the demise of the Co-operative movement in many areas of its business started to bite and the Supermarket closed. Again the site was redeveloped with B & Q taking the biggest part of the land, with Topps Tiles, plus others trying their luck taking the rest of the area.

B & Q opened a big new warehouse in Kay Street, so the Crompton Way store days were numbered. When B& Q left, it was the turn of The Range to take over the empty B & Q premises.

Going down the street we cross Nell Street named after Nell's Farm after which the street was named. On our left is the church and graveyard of St. Paul's.

ST. PAULS.

St Paul's parish was formed in 1844 out of the townships of Little Bolton and Sharples. Services were originally held at a Chapel of Ease at Ashgrove, Old Road., which had been licensed as a chapel. This was recorded in the London Gazette 3rd June 1844. Earl Wilton offered an acre of land for the building of the church. Canon James Slade was the overseer for the building of 11 churches in Bolton, St Paul's being one of them. Building started and on the afternoon of Thursday 22nd June 1848 The Bishop of Manchester consecrated the building. The cost was somewhere in the region of four thousand pounds. St Paul's first vicar was Rev. KA Fraser who had been the Curate in Charge at Ashbank Chapel. In 1859 Rev A Birley M. A. became the Vicar, followed in 1869 by Rev F Brindley M. A. both of whom had streets in the village named after them.

The Earl of Wilton again gave the church some land in Ivy bank Road on which to build a Vicarage. The St Paul's originally seated 745 souls of which 455 seats were free. In 1868 building started to enlarge the church. During this time the congregation went back to Ashbank. Unfortunately whilst the building work was going on, part of the roof collapsed killing one man and injuring two more. The enlarged church now seated 1,168. Originally there were no choir stalls in the chancel, these were introduced at a later date, and even then there were no marble screens. Theses were placed in memory of Rev. Lewis Reynolds Hearn who was the vicar at the time, unfortunately something happened and he fell from his stall whilst listening to the litany, and struck his head on the tiled floor, and unfortunately died the next day at the age of 73.

Sadly, as congregations started to fall, together with space being somewhat limited especially after the Parochial Hall at the top of Newnham Street was no longer available, alterations to the church's interior which would help the church to be more serviceable to the many groups using St Paul's were made.

The removal of some pews from the front of the church, and also under the gallery meant that the building was more flexible for other uses.

One great advantage was that of having a meeting room together with a kitchen under the balcony. Also there is an area at the front of the church which can be used for various activities. The church now seats around 500.

When I was a pupil at St. Paul's junior school, I, like many of the other pupils used the Children's Corner many times after leaving school in the afternoon. There were quite a number of books available, all I must say, with a Christian theme. We knew when it was time to go home when the verger started to hover around.

In the late 1800s and early 1900s St Paul's had a number of wealthy benefactors. One of which was the Thwaite family of

110

bleaching fame. The brass eagle lectern was given by Catherine Thwaite in Memory of her parents.

The organ was given by Thomas Thwaite who was the man responsible for the building of the Watermillock. The organ holds a mystery which I believe will never be solved. It was reported in the Bolton Evening News on 24th September 1965, that whilst workmen were busy restoring and rebuilding the organ, they discovered a number of pieces of old newspaper which must have been left there when the organ was originally built. There was a half page from the Sydney Morning Herald dated 10th November 1858 some thirteen years before the organ was built.

As I have already said how this came about we will never be certain. However I told a friend the story about the paper being found and he said that the old organ makers would wrap smaller wooden parts in newspaper to help keep them good and dry until the organ was being assembled, but why the Sydney Morning Herald I have no idea? I have had a look at the part of the paper, page 9 in fact, reported to have been found and all the information is about a summery of shipping arrivals and also foreign arrivals in Sydney.

Before the church had an organ, the hymns were led by a fiddle and a flute.

Frank Henry Denton was the organist and choirmaster for 35 years. He always came to church in a frock coat and a top hat. Another organist was one of the three famous B.B.C. Reginald's, namely Reginald Dixon, Reginald Forte and St Paul's Reginald Liversedge.

Reginald Liversedge was the resident organist at the Lido which opened on Easter Saturday 1937, with Jesse Matthews in the film "Evergreen".

During the interval Reginald seated at the organ a Christie 3/Manual /9 Rank Theatre Organ would rise out of the orchestra pit, playing popular tunes which the audience could sing too as the words were projected onto the big screen. On stage in the early days were Victor Snelson and his Orchestra.

Laurel and Hardy made one live appearance on 8th September 1947. The Inkspots also appeared live round about the same time. The lido was demolished in March 2006.

Reginald Liversedge became manager of the Regal Cinema in 1952, with the cinema changing its name to the Astor on 24th November 1952. On 9th November 1955 it opened as the Nevada Skating Rink with Mr Jack Winston on the organ.

At one service the wardens became aware of one of the congregation putting up an umbrella. Was it raining in?

The umbrella stayed up all the time. When the service ended the wardens approached the man enquiring about the umbrella, only to be told by the man that he was sitting in a draught and the umbrella shielded him from the draught.

In the 1930s the church had a robed mixed choir of both ladies and men of all ages including children from the primary school. The vestry is on the south side of the chancel and the ladies chapel on the north side. The war memorial remembering the people killed in the two world wars is the north wall.

In my day there was a very large Sunday school with all the classes meeting in the Parochial Hall.

Going to St Paul's as a lad in the 1930s & 40s was a little different to today. In those days you couldn't turn round to talk to the children behind you or one of the sidemen would come and tell you to sit facing the front and be quiet.

On Sermon Sunday all the able church members would walk in procession led by the Church Lads Brigade Band. We were always accompanied by at least two policemen who saw us safely across road junctions. The walk of witness would take somewhere around an hour, with stops for a word and hymn here and there. The route was up to a mile and we took a different route every year.

ST. PAULS SCHOOL

The first school and teacher's house were opened at the side of the church on the 21st June 1859 at a total cost of £2,198.
In 1871 a new school and lecture or parochial hall was built at the corner of Holland Street and School Street (now Newnham Street) at a cost of £1404. The Lecture Hall was upstairs. It was a square room about the size of a tennis court with a platform come stage at one side. During my time at St. Paul's it was very rarely used. There was a gate at the bottom of the stairs and the banister running up the stairs had brass studs about nine inches apart to stop lads from sliding down. The only time I have been in the hall was when our class were rehearsing for the Annual Bazaar.
Initially St. Paul's was a boy's school and it wasn't until 1881 that a girl's school was built on Blackburn Road costing £3,118, which is still standing although it is no longer a school. The boy's school and hall were demolished many years ago.
Over the years there have been many changes at St Paul's school and the buildings. The first building which was originally the girl's school became mixed infants school. The second building containing the hall was used as an infant's school for some time, and then became the class 1 in the primary school, with the Blackburn Road building from classes 2 to 4A.
Toilet facilities by today's standards were less than basic. The toilets in the infants department were outside in the playground and open to the weather. Whilst the primary school boy's toilets were covered, and also in the playground, they were very dark, damp, and dingy, in fact to a 7 to 10 year old a little scary.
The school caretaker's house was on Blackburn Road where the Royal Bank of Scotland now stands. I recall that children in the infant's school all used the same play ground which had two entrances. One in Holland Street, near the corner of Newnham Street, and the other near the infant's school building in

Newnham Street. Both of these entrances had iron gates which dragged on the floor due to children swinging on them.

In the infant's yard were some railed off steps to the cellar. Although the church was railed off all round, there was a passage way leading from the school into the church yard. This was used very rarely, mainly on Ascension Day when the children went to a special service. This saved the infants from going onto the streets.

In the 1930s the entrance to the school was through the playground, but prior to that the official entrance was from Newnham Street, the lintel over the door was carved Girl's School over the door. Here again I never remember this entrance to be used. On the roof was a small bell tower. As we go through the cloak room, we come into the reception classroom which was as wide as the building, from this room was the corridor leading to the church yard. The next classroom room was about half as long again as the first. This room doubled up first thing in the morning for assembly of the whole school. At the back of the building were two more classrooms side by side.

The primary school was on two sites. Class 1 was underneath the lecture hall with its own cloakroom and toilets. Classes 2 to 4B were in the bigger school.

The primary school had separate yards for both boys and girls. The girl's cloakroom was more spacious in comparison with the boys. However during the war part of the room was used for the collection of salvage which was collected for the war effort. There were three very large hessian bags each about three feet wide, which were hung on the coat hooks on a part of the cloakroom not used by the girls. One for paper and cardboard, one for tins and another for bones. Pupils would bring as much salvage as they could. Many lads would spend time knocking on doors after school asking, "Have you any salvage please"

The bags were collected once a fortnight.

In the Primary school there were four classrooms, and an assembly hall. Two of the classrooms were at the front of the hall and two at the back.

Class 2 was on the left as you looked at the school from Blackburn Road had a door which led to the headmaster's room and also one from the girls cloak room. There was also a door into class 2. Class 4A (some times referred too as the scholarship class) was on the right. Here again was a entrance from Blackburn Road. Class 3 was on the left, this room had a small entrance hall from the girl's playground which was very rarely used however it had on display some strange things in glass bottles. They were probably used when the school had pupils up to the age of 14. By coincidence I was taught by Miss Longworth who taught my father just over 26 years before. She must have been teaching at St Paul's for more than 30 years. On the right was class 4B. Like class 3 there was a small entrance hall from the boy's playground. There were sliding partitions between class 2 and class 4A, and also between these two classes and the assembly hall. This, when the partitions were folded back it doubled the size of the hall for special functions, such as plays, or schoolwork displays.

The school yard in the infants was paved, both the girls and boys yards in the primary school were cobbled.

At the start of every day we had morning assembly which lasted about 20 minutes, starting with a hymn, bible reading, a short word, and finally another hymn. Some of the favourite hymns chosen were. We plough the fields and scatter, Onward Christian soldiers, Fight the good fight, O Worship the King, etc.

Thursday morning assembly was always taken by the Vicar. In my time there the vicar was Canon Groves.

In some classrooms we had double desks with wrought iron frames with wooden seats and in others there were double desks with separate chairs. As you moved from the infants school to the primary school you were introduced to pen and ink, and each desk had a little ink well. The nibs on the pens were at times a bit scratchy and if you got too much ink on your pen you would finish up with a big blob of ink on the page of your exercise book. I am sorry to say that my exercise book was a real mess due to my being left handed as I would drag my hand over the undried ink smudging most of my work. Many left handed people write with their hand over and above where they are writing instead of alongside in the way done right handed people, this saves smudging top. The blue exercise books used to have all the various tables on the back page. For instance, arithmetic multiplication tables from 1 to 12, liquid measures, weight measures including poles, perches, and rods.

All pupils in the school belonged to one of four houses, with each house representing a colour, the houses were :-

BRIDGE   YELLOW
CHURCH   BLUE
PARK   GREEN
VALE   BLUE

Points were awarded for many things, good work, clean fingernails, tidy hair, good behaviour, etc. By the same token points were also deducted for being late, bad behaviour and so on. In P E pupils wore the coloured band of the house in which they were representing for team games. At the end of each week a Monitor would go round the school noting the number of points attained for the different houses which were usually recorded in the top corner of the class blackboard.

I cannot remember having prefects as we did in senior school. Usually at St Paul's scripture was the first subject every morning, and at the end of the first classroom period, there was a short break for milk. The milk came in small bottles and nearly every child had a bottle.

The subjects in my day were quite varied, Arithmetic, English, History, Geography. Physical Education, etc. and usually in some classes during the two last periods on Friday afternoon, pupils were allowed to bring in their own books to read. In class

116

4A our last two periods were spent at Moss Street Baths for swimming instructions. We went to the baths on the bus from Seymour Road at a cost of a halfpenny. Whilst there is now a bus stop outside the Royal Bank of Scotland in those days the stop did not exist. It was only introduced after the war.

A number of us when making our way home after swimming would call at the Naafipak café at the corner of Moss Street and Halliwell Road, for an unbuttered flour cake which cost a penny. The café building was an old Williams Deacons Bank. Some of us used to make our way across the road to the greengrocers, which was next to the Waterloo Hotel for a penny apple, and as it was wartime the apples were usually baking and quite sour.

Many schools today have field trips which can take them to many places far and wide, I remember our field trip from St Paul's was a 200 yard walk to be taken on a tour of John Ashworths mill in Holland Street. One thing I hated if we had something out of the ordinary, the following day we had to write an essay about what we had done.

Whilst discipline was fairly strict it was always fair, and I am glad to say the cane was not used a great deal.

One thing children worried about was their school report wondering what the teacher was going to say. Our reports started with each subject being listed in how well we had done percentage wise in the various tests. Some comments by the teachers were encouraging, whilst others had the opposite effect, such as "could do better"

Out side the school on Blackburn Road facing Walch's corn shop was a Belisha Beacon crossing which had a line of large top steel studs marking out the pedestrian crossing, and on each side of the road on the top of a black and white painted post was an orange flashing light, which was a warning to motorists of the pedestrian crossing. The Belisha beacon road crossing was the forerunner of our present day Zebra crossings. They were named after the transport minister of the time Hore Belisha who introduced them in the 1930s. The zebra crossing was brought in the 1950s.

When war broke out in 1939 gas masks were issued which for a time we carried with us every day. We had air raid drill although I cannot remember the sirens going during the day, but at night it was quite different as they sounded nearly every night for a number of years. In the early days of the war we would make our way to the air raid shelters, however although we were only twelve miles from Manchester and thirty miles from Liverpool both cities being bombed regularly, in Bolton we were quite fortunate as only a few bombs in comparison dropped on the town. After a few months majority of people ignored the sirens and stayed in bed.

Some time in 1937/38 the council decided to introduce secondary schools, as up to then the pupils stayed at the same school until they were old enough to start work, this was with the exception of people who passed for grammar school. Castle Hill in Tonge Moor was a new school built for this purpose with many other secondary schools being founded. Busses were laid on to ferry children from the Astley Bridge junior Schools to Castle Hill, for instance, Bank Top, Seymour Road Wesleyans and St Paul's. Holy Infant's pupils usually went to a Catholic secondary school. The children would assemble on some spare land at the side of Astley Bridge Library. The land is now a car park for the Conservative Club. There were two busses, each doing two journeys from Astley Bridge to Castle Hill. One for boys and one for girls. The first bus would leave at 8-20am and the second at 8-40am. By the way these journeys were free. Castle Hill school building had a Primary school, a senior boy's school, and a senior girl's school. Whilst all three departments were in the same building they were totally independent of one another. The school was a really modern building in its time, with nine classrooms, one was the only room on a second floor, the other eight were on the ground floor and had four sets of French windows on each side, which made it light and airy. There was a large hall and the headmasters study. I believe that the senior girl's school was of a similar layout.

The boys department was a three formed streamed intake. The classes were each given a letter with the streaming as follows E, B, C.

During the war pupils in their last year could help the war effort by spending two weeks potato picking. We had not to go far to pick potatoes as the field between Hall I'th Wood and Crompton Way had been cultivated for potatoes. There were about ten children, a farmer with his tractor, and three Women's Land Army Girls. We were paid for our work and an extra bonus was two weeks off school. After the war the field reverted to a meadow again.

There was a science laboratory, a woodwork room, a toy making room, a gymnasium, a vegetable allotment complete with a greenhouse.

There was one little problem with having to catch busses too and from school, and that was if the class was a bit naughty we would be kept in for 15 minutes after school time, consequently we missed the bus and had to walk home. One lad in our class seemed to be the main culprit for our detention, he was liked by everyone and he had a sort of love hate relationship with our teacher Miss Green, so much so, we have seen her laugh and also been close to tears at his antics.

Had the war not stated in 1939 the school would have had a swimming pool, however in its place air raid shelters were built. The school had houses similar to St Paul's

NEWTON -- RED
CROMPTON – GREEN
LISTER—BLUE
LIVINGSTONE -- YELLOW

The school had its own football pitch; however it had a bonus of around a dozen council owned pitches on Hall i'th Wood playing fields, which were nearby. During the war and many years after the war ended Castle hill as a secondary school had come to the end of its life and closed.

Motto, As strong as a castle, as bright as a star, and as busy as a bee.

ST. PAUL'S PAROCHIAL HALL

In the earlier part of the 20th century St Paul's Astley Bridge was
a very active and thriving church, with a large congregation.
There were many wealthy benefactors in its flock, and in 1914.
It was decided that the church needed more facilities for its
members. Land was acquired on Almond Street at the top of
Newnham Street, and the building of a parochial hall was
started. A lot of thought about what the church, its people, and
the area needed was put into the project.

A unique feature about the new hall was the laying of four
foundation stones, one each by Col TM Hesketh, Walter Mather,
Percy Ashworth, and Arthur S Holmes.

This was to be, and was probably the best church halls in the
county.

The hall had a purpose built theatre complete with sloping floor
and tip up seats, with a reasonable sized stage, and three small
dressing rooms at the rear. There was also a large hall which
was used for many functions, such as Wedding Receptions,
dances, social gatherings, bazaars, gym and keep fit. It was used
by the Church Lads Brigade which had up to 80 members for
band practice and other activities. This was a great asset to a
very busy church. The hall had a fully furnished industrial sized
kitchen capable of catering for any function, be it a coffee
morning, or a three course meal.

On the left as you faced the front of the building was a large
room containing two full sized billiard tables, and on the right
was quite a large meeting room, in fact it was the same size as
the billiard room. Between the two rooms were two double door
entrances, with another probably false door between. Usually
only one entrance was used as the foyer behind the south
entrance was used as a storage space for spare chairs. The false
door was covering the staircase to the second floor. The foyers
from both the entrances led to a largish welcoming foyer. This

area was the sort of hub for the front part of the hall which led to the billiard room and also the large meeting room opposite. The men's cloakroom and toilet, and also a small storage/meeting room were off the foyer..

As you made your way further into the hall, the main corridor which was about 9 to 10 feet wide led you between the kitchen on one side and the ladies cloakroom and toilets on the other. Here you came to a cross road to the right was the entrance to the kitchen, and a double entrance to the main hall or function room. On the right was another corridor leading to entrance to the theatre, on this corridor was an emergency exit. The theatre itself had three exits, two at the back and one leading into the main corridor near to the stage.

The function room had two exits one I have already mentioned and another facing the theatre exit. The exits were also used as entrances. Further down the main corridor was the stage door to the dressing rooms and at the end of the corridor was a double exit door to the rear of the building.

The theatre was used not only for St Paul's productions, but also many other operatic, and drama societies, such as Sweetloves and another very popular one was the New Rosemere Operatic Company which was renowned for their great Gilbert and Sullivan productions. They first used the hall in 1943.

A great drawback many societies had with some of their productions was that dressing room accommodation was inadequate. This problem was overcome by dividing the main corridor from the stage door to the bottom doors of the function room with a temporary heavy curtain, and again in the function room an area was curtained off to give more dressing room facilities.

Whilst most of the Parochial Hall was single story the front part had a second floor, with a stair case which led from the north side foyer behind the false front door. It led to a corridor with two large meeting rooms and two smaller storage rooms. All the rooms were used for Sunday school classrooms and during the week for a host of other activities.

At the rear of the building were some steps leading from the hall to a bowling green and beyond the green was a tennis hut with changing rooms, complete with tennis courts. Usually Tuesday night was maintenance night when the courts were rolled and freshened up. The whole setup was very impressive.

Down one side of the hall was a driveway sheltered with trees, whilst on the other side was a footpath belonging to the hall, again, sheltered with trees. There was also another footpath which ran parallel to the halls. This led to a guinnel which went to Seymour Road.

The hall was very well used during the evening with the billiard room being well supported; many church groups met weekly and as I have already said the Church Lads Brigade used the building at least once a week.

St Paul's held an annual Bazaar around November, when every group in the church would help to raise money towards the running cost of the church and buildings. The Function hall was set up like an open market with stalls down both sides and in the middle. All the different groups taking stall to sell all sorts of goods, some made by members and others donated.

The Bazaar was always opened in the theatre by pupils from the day school. The concert lasted some where in the region of an hour, with short plays, recitations, choirs and instrumentalists showing their prowess playing the instrument of their choice.

I remember my last year at St Paul's. Mr Carter the Headmaster had managed to get hold of some bamboo, how he did this I do not know. The war had been going for two years and every thing was in short supply or not available at all. Anyway, we had the bamboo and with Mr Carter's help 14 of us made recorders out of the tube. We rehearsed in the old church hall above standard one, which I have already said has long since gone. I hazard to think what the 14 of us sounded like on these untuned home made instruments. It probably sounded like a cat chorus.

The Bazaars were always well supported and for many years around £1000 pounds was raised. By today's standards this would be about £20,000.

Unfortunately the building was used very little through the day during the week, and it was reported in the Bolton Evening News on 15th November 1937 that the Rev Canon P Groves the vicar of St Paul's, suggested that the hall be used as a junior school. He went on to say, "That during the evening it was a hive of industry, but it was a white elephant during the day." It was estimated that £6,000 would be needed for the scheme, and it was decided to defer the decision for three years, and as the war intervened nothing happened.

One big problem with a project like the Parochial Hall is the cost of maintenance, and from being a great asset in its early days, after the war it became a great liability. A lot of the wealthy benefactors had passed on and were no longer around to help. Sadly the hall was demolished and the land used for housing.

Many people will fondly remember going to the hall to see a play or musical, maybe a dance or party. I was a member of the Church Lads Brigade whose motto was, "Fight the good fight" We had at least one Company night every week meeting in the Parochial Hall. The evening would be filled with various activities such as drill practice, keep fit, indoor games; chalk rugby was a favourite, and there was plenty of badge work.

The Company also had a band containing buglers, drummers, and needless to say a big drum player which met for practice sometimes on a different night to the rest of the Company. To get into the band was not easy as there was a waiting list for members. There was a church parade once a month where the band would lead the Company on a half hour march within the Parish before going into the church for the service. The march took a different route each month.

124

St Paul's CLB Company was well supported with some 60 plus members in the 1930s and 40s. Its chief officer was Col Clarckson. As time went by the numbers of members started to drop, and eventually St Paul's Company joined with All Souls Company in Astley Street, but sadly the numbers kept dropping and the amalgamated Company disbanded.

The last few minutes of each Company night there was a bible reading and the CLB prayer.

'Heavenly Father, bless and guide with your spirit the work of the Church Lads' and Church Girls' Brigade. Help us never be ashamed to confess the faith of Christ crucified. To fight valiantly under his banner against sin, the world and the devil, and to continue as his faithful soldiers and servants to the end of our lives. Amen'

Talbot Street and Brindley Terrace run from Newnham Street to Nell Street. Brindley Terrace, like Murton Terrace is a bit unique as being two of the very few thoroughfares with just a foot path at the front.

Two of the old schools buildings are still in use, one as a Cash and Carry and the other I believe a Restaurant. The new school stands on land once known as Berry Fold on which was built The beeches. Many years before the new school was built ther also stood on the land Mr Hough's blacksmith's shop. He would let schoolchildren stand at the door whilst he made and fitted shoes to horses.

St. Paul's present school was opened in 1967.

As we return to Seymour Road we pass "The 12 shops" a nickname for this parade of shops in the 20s and 30s. There have been many changes to the types of businesses in this row over the past 100 years. At the turn of the 20th century there were 2 greengrocers, a barbers, 2 confectioners, a bootmaker, a painter, a post office, a butcher, a hardware shop, a chemist, and also a chapel keeper lived in the row. Changes over the next 30 years, were considerable. The Barbers shop became a confectioners, the other confectioners was take over by Young's a local multiple confectioners, the chapel keepers house became Mercers newsagents, eventually owned by Reginald Liversedge, who incidentally had a grand piano in the front upstairs room. The piano was easily seen from the top deck of the bus as the bus stop was nearby. The post office was taken over by S R Walsh the overall manufacturer who started business in the mid 1800s. And the post office being transferred to Knott's Chemist, the butchers became a temperance bar, the hardware shop became confectioners and then a gramophone shop, the bootmaker became Vose's tripe shop, and 1 greengrocer became a draper. So there have been quite a lot of changes over the past 30 or so years. Sometime in the early 1950s there was a radio and television shop in the row. One night around 8-30pm a van drew up outside the shop and two men in long white coats went into the shop and virtually cleared the stock. I suppose any passers by who saw the men especially in white coats would never think that they were thieves. I don't remember the final outcome of the robbery. Looking back over the years there has been quite a turnover of trades and businesses in this row of shops.

As we cross Blackburn Road to the Lamb Hotel there is macadam covering the carriageway. This macadam was laid just after the last war. It covers the previous road surface of granite sets. There were two types of sets. The sets within the tramlines and about a foot outside tramlines were of different granite from the rest. The tramline sets had ahint of green whilst the rest were grey.

Just higher up Blackburn Road than the Lamb Hotel is another parade of shops which like the "twelve shops" have changed hands and commodities over the last hundred of years or so.
At the end of the last war in the first row from the Lamb was a gent's tailor, a confectioner, an ironmonger, Smith's hairdresser,

Maypole, Johnson Lord Tobacconist, *Argentine Meat Company*.
Who did a "special" every Thursday lunchtime of sliced beef
and gravy, Misses F&E Lumb a milliner', and finally the
Radcliffes wardrobe and furniture shop.
In the next Block was Miss Halliwell's grocery shop,
Unsworth's tripe shop, a private house followed by Walsh's
Corn Shop. In the gap between the shops came a lovely cottage
facing south with an equally lovely garden, the highlight of
which was the great apple tree in the middle.
Just past this house and garden were a number of stone premises
including a private house, a fish and chip shop which at one
time belong to Leach's then taken over by Donald and Charlotte
Fielding who eventually took over the leadership of Lee Clough
Mission, Donald took over as Pastor for many years until he
passed away in 2012 having lost Charlotte some time before.
Next door was a tripe shop, followed by an electricians.
Street directories from before 1932 show more and a different
mix of house and shops than the ones I remember.

Crossing Penny Brow, and sometime before the arrival of Asda
stood T M Heskeths and Sons, New Mills, which were built on
land known as Hills Fold. There were three mills in total.
Building started in 1866; however who owned them between
1866 and 1884 is something of a mystery as John Stone and
Company appeared to start business in 1884 with the Hesketh
family taking over in 1990. In 1950 they joined the Crosses and
Heaton group, and as business declined the mils finally closed.
The mill was the first in the country to install sprinkler system.
In a separate building alongside penny brow were offices and a
canteen, and alongside Blackburn Road were more up market
offices.

HESKETH'S MILL

A sad occasion in the early 1900s was that a young child drowned in the mill lodge. The child's father was a mill manager. The Bolton News dated 3rd November 2012 reported that the farmer from Harricroft Farm stored silage which contaminated Heskeths lodge killing hundreds of fish which was around 90% of the lodges stock. The farmer had already been find £8,000 plus £2866 costs and agreed a further out of court settlement of £10,000 to the Bolton Co-operative Angling Club to restock the lodge

NUMBER TWO MILL AFTER EXTENSION

The northern boundary of the mill property was on Heywood Street, which was renamed Cavendish Street in around 1901/2 which in turn became Moss Bank Way in 1938.

COL GEORGE HESKETH

Born 30th August
Died 30th April 1930 in the Fylde
Chairman of T M Hesketh and Son's
Youngest son of founder Thomas Manley Hesketh
He was the first and only chairman of Astley Bridge Urban District Council 1838-1887
His brother Col Thomas Hesketh had earlier been chairman of Astley Bridge Local Board.
Represented Astley Bridge ward in 1895
Mayor of Bolton 1905-1906
His wife Minnie Mayoress
Opened Astley Bridge Park 27th April 1901
County Magistrate
Made Freeman of Bolton 25th July 1927
Appointed High Sherriff of Lancashire 1918

Like most of the mills in Bolton T M Heskeths closed and the site was cleared. There was talk of a multi story hotel, and other enterprises being built on the land. Time went by and nothing happened. The area was derelict with nature taking over. The whole place was an eyesore. Many locals complained, and then Asda came along and built a superstore on the land.

The new store opened on Tuesday 18th May 1970. In its early days there was a tyre bay, D I Y including timber, wallpaper and paint, and also a café. Some time later the café went together with the tyre bay, and also many of the DIY items, and the store extended.

However, it was many years after opening their store that Asda finally acquired a piece of property to partly complete their operation in Astley Bridge, and that was a shop building on Blackburn Road after which the Petrol station was moved across the car park to its present site.

Asda work with the community work with many projects in Astley Bridge they support many charities and local schools efforts.

The store was involved together with seven local schools and other volunteers including David Crausby the local M P and John Walsh one of the three Astley Bridge councillors in the Town Tidy up Campaign. Over 300 people were involved in a litter picking exercise. The Mayor and Mayoress Guy and Collette Harkin came to show their support.

WHERE DID PEOPLE COME FROM TO MAN THE MILLS?

When Eagley, and New Eagley mills were built, the former in 1796, and the latter in 1802-3 where did the workers come from and how were they all trained? In Astley Bridge there were only 873 people, most of whom would be farmers and farm hands. We know that many people came off the land to work in the mills, and also many came from Ireland but where did they stay. If we look at some of the older property in Astley Bridge we find that building houses did not really start in earnest until 1830, and these were built of stone.

Skrike Fold   Late 1700
Whitehill Cottages Belmont Road early 1800
Maxwell Street   early 1800
Andrew Lane   1830
Pemberton Street   1830
Park Row   1830-40
Ashworth Lane   1840
Eleanor Street   1840
Hugh Lupose Street   1840
Cottages which became Bank Top church   1840
Playfair Street   1840-50
Birley Street   1850

There were also quite a lot of farms around at the time such as Bank Top, Cubbins, Fernhill, Gale, Harricroft, High Homes, Horrocks Fold, Moss Lea, New House, Oldhams, Old Nells, Sharples Hall, and others.
Probably a number of these farms have interesting histories such as Gale farm which is overlooked by Horrocks Moor. Mr Moxom and his wife came from Yorkshire. The Journal of 15th July 1955 reported that they had been there for thirty years, and

that the farm was reputed to be part of a Nunnery, with three pieces of evidence supporting the idea.

The coal house was supposed to be the bake house. One wall shows the existence of a chimney and an open grate. The barn has a number of cells each with its own tiny windows. Under the kitchen in the cellar are some stone steps leading to a dark and cold room with an arched stone roof. Also there is another small room where Irish labourers slept during haymaking time.

It makes you wonder what other stories can be told about these old farmhouses.

I also wonder where all the money came from to pay for the building of the many mills, not only in Astley Bridge but also Bolton and the other Lancashire towns. Another puzzle is where did all the building tradesmen come from, the Bricklayers, joiners, plumbers and other tradesmen. We know that many men came over from Ireland to work as labourers. There is not only the cost of the buildings but also plus all the equipment and machinery required.

When the early mills were built labour could possibly be scarce, that is until many people heard that there was work aplenty. People moved from working on farms into the towns in their thousands, also many Irish people came to work in the mills.

Initially training both men and women would be a formidable task with so many processes from the raw cotton coming into the mill and processed to the finished product.

The raw cotton would arrive in bales which were broken open, then willowing which is the breaking up of raw cotton, followed by the scutcher which removed impurities. The cotton then went to the Card room where it was carded meaning disentanglement of the fibres. The cotton went on to the combing machines, followed by the draw frames, on to the slubbers which prepares the cotton for spinning.

Many cotton workers wore clogs, however many would work in their bare feet especially in the spinning room where the floor could be very oily. Some of the women would change their shoes as soon as they got into the card room, usually into an old pair which were known as trashers.

When the mills engine started up, the great driving shafts which went from one end of the card or spinning rooms to the other started to rotate, in turn this would drive the pulleys which powered the machines. The pulleys were quite dangerous as should some loose clothing or even a persons arm got caught with the pulley belt, a person could loose an arm or even their life.

When the mills were in full swing whole families would be employed by the same mill. The adults would be working full time, and many of their children working part time. In the early eighteen hundreds, children as young as four were employed as scavengers. Scavengers were the lowest of the apprentices. They were employed to work under moving machinery to clean up the dust, oil the machinery, and gather cotton that had been thrown by the spinning mule as it moved back and forth.

A little piercer's job was to gather up and piece up all the loose ends as the mules moved backward and forward. It was estimated that a little piercer walked backwards and forward for between 20 and 24 miles a day

In 1818 George Gould wrote, a five year old child was paid 1/6 per week, probably for 60 hours, if the child was older it would be paid more. As time went by things went a little better. In 1933 a new factory act was passed stating that a child between 9 and 13 could only work a nine hour day. In 1844 a new act limited the hours of 8 to 13 year olds to a six and a half hour day.

Girls would start probably as a "half timer" they were called tenters. My mother worked half time at 12 years old. Usually the women would work on one type of machine such as, a carding, or drawing machine (box tenter) however many women could work on most of the machines in the card room.

Cotton was taken from one process to another in cans, hence the expression "carrying the can", also card rooms and to a greater extent weaving sheds were very noisy, so noisy in fact, the workers had to lip read, or mee mawing. Norman Evans and also Les Dawson used mee mawing in some of their comedy routines, as they emphasised their words with their mouth.

Most of the mill workers were on piece work, which means they made their own wage. They only got paid for the cotton they produced.

Spinners were the cream of the crop as far as work was concerned. They were on the highest wage. Unfortunately in the 1800s and early 1900s they were over the hill when they reached 40, and they lost their job. Some philanthropist mill owners would try to find them a labourer's job but many spinners finished up on the scrap heap.

Child workers in mills were known as "white slaves" because they worked longer hours, and in many cases in worse conditions than the black slaves in America. Many children were maimed by losing fingers or arms, and in certain cases were killed by the machines.

CROMPTONS SPINNING MULE

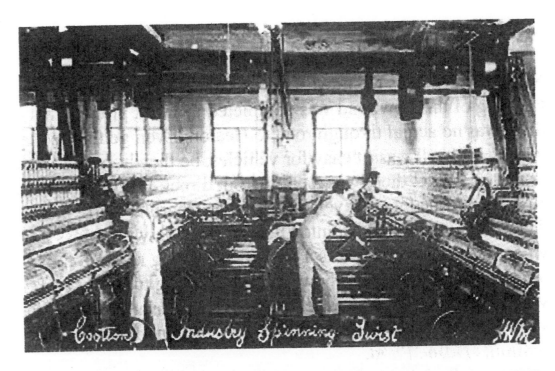

MULES IN THE SPINNING ROOM NOTE THE DRIVE SHAFT AND PULLEYS

CANS USED IN THE COTTON INDUSTRY (CARRYING THE CAN)

136

MOSS BANK WAY

Moss Bank Way is the newest main road in Astley Bridge. The building of this new road was completed in 1938, prior to this there was no actual through road to Heaton. Even getting to the top of Halliwell wasn't easy for vehicles, be they horse and carts or motor. To get there was anything but direct. From Blackburn Road you turned into Cavendish Street to Sharples Park, past Thornleigh, then left turn into Oldhams lane down to Moss Lea where there was, and still is a cart track, turning right up the track to Harricroft farm where you do a dog leg turn past two very old cottages one of which had a hand imprint on one of the stones near the door. Turn left past the Coaching House onto Smithills Deane Road.

Should you be walking at the crossroads of Sharples Park and the top of Berkely Road there was a foot path on the left taking you towards what was Eden's Orphanage. The footpath then turned right which was called by the locals the "mile o' boards" which was a very long and high solid wooden fence. As you walked alongside the fence it seemed to go for miles. At the end was Moss Lea where you could take a footpath which led you to a jiggling bridge over the brook to Temple Road which in it turn brought you to the top of Halliwell.

To try not to cause confusion, before the 1900s Heywood Street went from Blackburn Road to the junction of Broad O'th Lane and Sharples Park, When Astley Bridge joined Bolton the name Heywood Street was changed to Cavendish Street and it wasn't until 1938 that there was a connecting road from Halliwell to the Broad O'th Lane/Sharples Park junction and then onto Blackburn Road when Cavendish Street by name only became a memory.

On Cavendish Street were the Public Offices dating from 1896 which replaced the old Astley Bridge Council Offices at 548 Blackburn Road. Later this address was better known as Doctor Cranna's surgery.

PUBLIC OFFICES OPENED 1896

The Farnworth journal dated Saturday 20th May 1876 reported that the health of the district during the past month had been satisfactory, one death from whooping cough, four from chest infections two from convulsions in children and one from kidney disease, the returns for March one from typhoid, one from small pox six from chest infections, and five from convulsions.

Behind the public offices was the Astley Bridge Maintenance Yard until 1948 when it eventually became EBM wholesale building supplies.

During the last war an Air Raid Wardens Post was built on the Blackburn Road side of the Public Offices. The post was usually occupied by volunteer Air Raid Wardens who patrolled the streets during air raids and in the hours of darkness, they made sure that everyone's blackouts were secure. Should a light be showing the standard "put that light out" was shouted to the offender. As a lad I remember going into the ARP post which seemed to be quite cosy. The wardens had a carpet square which had seen better days the floor. There was also a second hand settee, table and chairs. The wardens were volunteers and spent some time in the Post when they weren't patrolling the streets. They were also responsible for directing civilians to the air raid shelters.

From 1900 part the Public Offices housed the library; this was until the new Carnegie library was built next door, which opened on 29th September 1910. It was paid for by Mr Carnegie. As was Halliwell and Great Lever libraries which also opened on the same day.

ASTLEY BRIDGE LIBRARY

The foundation stone of Astley Bridge library was laid by Alderman Horridge on 29th September 1909.

Mr Archibald Sprake came to Bolton as Chief Librarian in 1904; on his arrival he was not at all happy with the organisation, but also on the choice of books.

He started to re-organise the library operation and Astley Bridge was to be the guinea pig for the exercise. He got plenty of brickbats with his plans, however attitudes changed as the success of the project came good, and as a result Bolton became a training ground for librarians. Sadly whilst the building is still standing the library closed on Thursday 5th April 2012.

In the review of 2011, we are told that the annual cost of the library was £67,956, there were 80,346 transactions, made up of 26,550 visitors, 11,542 enquiries, and 42,254 issues. The cost per transaction was 85p. The total book stock was 14,797.

I have been a member of Astley Bridge library since about 1935 and in that time I have seen a number of changes in the layout. The library was originally in three sections, the reading room, the adults department, and the children's department.

I went to St. Paul's School and I remember going straight to the library from school. In those days after 4 o'clock the children used a different entrance to the adults. department and usually the desk was staffed with one of the more junior assistants, who carried the boxes of children's library book cards and tickets from the main desk to the children's desk ready for business

"SILENCE PLEASE" notices were displayed in all sections of the building. It did not pay to make a noise as the assistants would give you a hard stern glare followed by a "shush" and "be quiet."

One memory I have is that of being intrigued by the large map of Astley Bridge which in those days hung on the wall opposite to where it is now in the entrance hall. It was much higher on the wall which I feel was much better as the more populated parts of the village were nearer to eye level. Today, if you want to look at what was the centre of the village 50 to60 years ago you have to get down on your knees. I use the map as a very good bible of the boundary of the Astley Bridge village, as it was drawn up in 1911when Mr. Archibald Sparke was the Chief Librarian and as I have already said his attention to detail was second to none.

The reading room which is now the main body of the library was a "no go" area for children if unaccompanied. However on the few occasions I managed to peep into the room I was fascinated with the slanting desks which held mainly broadsheet newspapers. The newspapers were fastened to the desks by highly polished brass rod.

Also available were various magazines in special folders. These were usually found on the many tables in the reading room. One thing that I do remember was that during the day, especially in winter, were a number of men who were out of work, or retired not only enjoyed reading the newspapers but also meeting up with their friends for a quiet chat in a nice warm room.

ASTLEY BRIDGE LIBRARY READING ROOM

Outside the library was a very wide pavement in what became

Next to the library was a piece of derelict land facing Manley Terrace, I just wonder should there have been another terrace facing the existing one, if so what happened, did the builder go bankrupt.

Astley Bridge Park opened in 1901, whilst not being a large park, it is well used. In the 30s, the children's playground had swings, a helter skelter slide, rocking horse, swings, and a couple of other roundabouts. The play area has been upgraded all the old equipment has gone.

There were two well used tennis courts, both of which have gone, one became a basket ball court whilst the other was demolished and grassed over. Sometimes when you went to the office which was in the bowling green pavilion to book and hire a court there could be a waiting time of two hours to get on the courts. There always seemed to be a park keeper on hand taking payment for both tennis and bowls. There was no extra charge fire the hire of the bowls the cost was included in the price per hour. There was a large grassed play area and still is, suitable for football, cricket, rounders, and many other games. The bowling green was sacrosanct to the older men, in 1930s and 40s there did seem to be a clique amongst some of the bowling fraternity. If we as teenage lads had to wait for an hour for a tennis court, we would spend some time on the bowling green. Some of the bowlers thought that we were pains in the neck, and looking back I can understand why.

The reason was that we had no idea about the bias on the bowls, we could not read the green and more often than not, would bowl quite short which left our woods in the middle of the green much to the annoyance of some of the bowlers because we were spoiling their game. One or two of the older men would kindly come over and try to teach us how to bowl. One thing that the crown green bowlers did that impressed people, and I believe that they are still doing it today, and that is when a funeral passes they stop bowling and face the cortege as it passes should any of the bowlers be wearing a hat they will take it off, which showed a great mark of respect.

The park was a good well patronised outdoor community centre and was a great asset to the people both young and old. Sometimes the lads would sort themselves out into two teams put their coats down as goal posts and get on with a game of football. The girls would do a similar thing when playing rounders; they would use their coats as corner posts.

 At the entrance to the park the flower beds were filled with a lovely display of colourful flowers. There were also some forms facing the flowers where usually you found the older people sitting and enjoying the scene. On many occasions these people would be licking an ice cream cornet or a slider (today we call them wafers.) which they had bought from the ice cream cart standing just outside the park gates.

COLOURFUL FLOWER DISPLAYS

The park keeper's house was on the corner of Cavendish Street and Broad O'th Lane. One amazing thing about the park keepers was that if a child was a little mischievous by walking on the grass, which had a little notice "Keep off the Grass" the park keeper seemed to come out of the woodwork to tell the child off.

HOLY INFANTS AND ST. ANTHONYS

After the war, a piece of the park was taken to build a new Roman Catholic Holy Infants School which opened in1965, and was extended in 1972. This area was known as Spring Bank where a number of cottages used to stand.

On Wednesday 9th August 1848 the Catholics celebrated the opening of a new church in Salford, St John the Evangelist. There were many bishops and priests and a congregation of about 1,600 in attendance.

Pope Pius 1X re-established the Catholic Diocese on 29th September 1850. On 25th July 1851 St. John the Evangelist church in Salford was made a Cathedral when the first bishop Doctor William Turner a Lancastrian from Whittingham was consecrated, he died whilst in office on 13th July 1872. The current Bishop is the Right Reverend Terence John Brain. He was appointed Bishop of Salford 2nd September 1997.

Before Holy Infants and St Anthony was built, Astley Bridge and other areas in north Bolton were in the parish of St Mary's in Palace Street. This was a large parish, and the journey from

Astley Bridge to Palace Street was not easy especially for the more elderly people.

In winter it would be very difficult to make the journey. Trams did not start to operate until the 1880s, and only the more wealthy people would own a pony and trap, but even so St Mary's was bursting at the seams.

J A Hilton tells us in his book "Catholic Lancashire" that the Irish immigrant population between 1841 & 51 nearly doubled to over 191,000, and in1851 17% of Manchester's population were Irish. However by 1881 the figure was down to 7.5%, this wasn't because many of them had left but probably because of an influx of people coming from the rural and country areas to work in the booming city.

It was decided to build a chapel of ease in Astley Bridge, which opened 22nd August 1877. This was a big help to many Roman Catholic worshipers.

In 1874 a plot of land was bought for £47 which at one time was a brick yard and a new school and chapel were built. The new mission of Holy Infants and St Anthony was born. The first priest was Fr Maximillion who lived at Park View. Times were bad for the parishioners who were few and very poor.

In its day the new chapel filled its roll, and in 1882 the day school started. In the schools early days the children could start work half time at ten tears old. In November 1934 there was an epidemic of scarlet fever; In November 1936 the fog was so bad the school was closed. In 1940 heavy snow caused a poor attendance with only 94 pupils attending on the Monday, but this dropped to just 34 on the Tuesday, so the school closed for the rest of the week. The building was three stories high with the bottom being a covered a playground, the next floor was the school, and the third floor was the chapel.

As more mills and other forms of industry came to the village there was an influx of people to work in the new industries. In 1894 Fr A M Vantonne came to the chapel and during his time the church was built and opened in 1902. A nice gesture in recognition of his work by the council was to name an Astley Bridge street after him. With the building of the church, it meant that the school could use more of the building.

However with Astley Bridge people, and housing increasing in number, there was a need for a new school. Not only was the old school too small, but the facilities were out dated and needed replacing. The new school was built after the war. The old building was taken down and the area is now used as a car park. When you look at the site where the old building stood in its latter days, you get the impression what a small area the building covered and also the feeling that there must have been plenty of overcrowding.

The rows of terraced houses in Mitre Street, and one side of Baxendale Street are still standing, but the terraced houses on Drummond Street, Major Street, Warwick Street, Baber Street, Maxwell Street, and the east side of Baxendale Street have all been demolished. As too was the Belle cinema which was destroyed by fire.

I remember that just before the war, the terrace of red brick houses in Maxwell Street were condemned, however due to the war, the houses were saved and I believe that they were taken off the condemned list. A landlord who owned most, if not all the houses sold all he owned for £50 each. A lot of the houses realised over a thousand pounds when resold.

On the land now stands 52 Bungalows (1, 2, &3 bedrooms) built in 1985 and houses people aged 60 and over. There is a community centre with lounge and garden. Some meals are available which are cooked on premises, a community alarm system, and regular social activities. The bungalows are rented and the organisation responsible is "Bolton at Home".

On the north west corner of what was T M Heskeths mills is now Hillview Court. Which comprises of a number of apartment blocks and houses. Running between Hillview Court and the

146

Asda supermarket is Hillview Road and on this road is a branch of the HSBC Bank.

There is also an area for the collection of bottles, tins, paper and cloths for recycling.

HESKETH'S LODGE AND HILLVIEW COURT

The building of Moss Bank Way caused a fair amount of disruption with the addition of two extra carriageways.

I have already mentioned Astley Bridge Cricket Club and the Thorns losing land. Also the end house in Manley Terrace and Williams Deacons Bank on Blackburn Road were bought by compulsory purchase in order to facilitate road widening

The bank relocated on the opposite side of Blackburn Road. Pavements were moved back in front of the park, library, and the public offices.

Eventually further improvements were needed to the busy crossroads of Blackburn Road and Crompton Way/ Moss Bank Way, and a number of buildings on the west of Blackburn Road had compulsory purchase orders on them. The Grapes Inn, Astley bridge Conservative Club which relocated with a new building on derelict land facing Manley Terrace, The Co-op

Boot and shoe shop. Wilkinson's greengrocers. a sweet shop and a dry cleaners, a private Boot and Shoe shop, and a Grocers Shop.

There is now a small car park where some of these buildings stood, many people do not realise that it is there as there is no direct access from Moss Bank Way. To use the car park you have to turn off Moss Bank Way into Drummond Street or Manley Terrace, then right into Warwick Street towards Belmont Road then right again down a back street just after the electricity sub station.

BELMONT ROAD

We continue our journey up the west side of Belmont Road. Due to the crossroad alteration the first house on this side was demolished. The old Co-op branch number 12 stands at the corner of Warwick Street, it is now a bookies, next door was the Co-op butchers followed by stone cottages some of which were taken down when the Drummond Street community bungalows were built. The row of bungalows facing Belmont Road had a garden with lawn and bushes, unfortunately the gardens were a dumping ground for cans and bottles, and also fast food waste. Due to this nuisance a high "see through" metal fence was built with a gateway in the middle.

A very decorative wrought iron gate was made; the theme of this gate is a sort of potted history of this area of the village. The initials of D. S. R. A. denoting Drummond Street Residents Association.
The motto on the gate is "Gang Warily" which is the motto of the Drummond Clan. The motto means "Go Carefully"
The Films and Cans remind us of the Belle Cinema.
The Birds depict the ducks and swans on Hesketh's and Ashworth's Lodges
The Dancers represent frequent dances at St Paul's Parochial Hall, and Bank Top School each Saturday evening during the winter months. There was an official opening of the new gate by the Mayor Mr John Walsh in 2002.
At the end of the row of cottages was the Belle cinema yard.

THE BELLE CINEMA

This was the entrance to the Belle Electric Theatre as it was called when it opened on 12th August 1914, seating 580, however the number of seats were reduced due to alterations. It was classed as a category 4 cinema which was next to the bottom of the pile in cinema classifications. The Empire in Howard Street was the only category 5 cinema in Bolton which meant that the films could be up to 2 years old before being shown at the Empire.

New films were shown first at category 1 cinemas like the Odeon, Lido, and the Capitol (ABC) then were passed to category 2 and so on. As said previously the Belle closed in 1957 after a disastrous fire.

The main picture was changed three times a week. Many people like me would call at the local shop for toffee's, and maybe cigarettes. Sometimes we would not bother going into the shop but put our pennies in the chewing gum machine which was on the wall usually at the side of the shop door. Even in those days there were special offers, as most of the machines gave a free packet of chewing gum with every fourth packet bought, be it P.K or Beech Nut.

During the week, the programmes were continuous, but on Saturday night there were two separate houses. One started around six o'clock, and the second about eight fifteen. As teenagers we were always second house fans which meant queuing well before the second house starting time. When the films had been box office successes we would queue all the more earlier. Once inside the format was similar to the town centre cinemas except for the decor, especially the seats. The first few rows of seats were a little austere with little or no padding. Mind you the price was only four pence (gradely money not metric). The bulk of the seats behind the cheap ones were more comfortable with more padding and some springs, they would cost you sixpence. Then came the dearer seats costing ten pence. Also, right at the back of the Belle just below the projection room was a raised boxed shaped seating area which was sort of on its own, as a passageway came between the main seating area and the raised seats. If you sat in this area you paid the best seat price of ten pence. At many cinemas where all the seats have been taken, the management would allow people to stand at the back, when seats became vacant the first in the line would be shown to seats whilst the people in the line moved up. This could not happen at the Belle because of the box area. Soon after the war the prices went up to, if my memory serves me correctly, Sixpence, Ninepence and a Shilling.

One of the features of not only the local cinemas but also the one's in town were the double seats on the back row. Quite a must for the courting couples. Whether these people ever watched the film or not I will leave it to your imagination. Having bought your ticket you entered the theatre, an usherette would tear the ticket into halves, one half was returned to you which as proof of purchase whilst the other half would be put on a spike holding some cord and in turn the half ticket was pushed down the cord.

Should you enter the cinema when the programme had started the auditorium would be quite dark as your eyes had not adjusted to the darkness. There was second usherette who would show you to a seat with the aid of a torch. The empty seat always seemed to be in the middle of the row which meant that you had to be careful not to stand on people's feet.

Until the smoking ban many people had a cigarette whilst watching a film, there were ashtrays on the backs of the seats in front of people, and the air could get thick with smoke. This was very noticeable as you looked up at projection rays of the film. As I have said earlier some of the films were over a year old or more and had had a lot of wear and tear, consequently from time to time they would break leaving a blank screen. Needless to say this usually happened in a very interesting or gripping part of the picture. I suppose at these times the animal instinct took over and every one would first gasp "awe" then started to stamp their feet. In no time at all the house lights came up and there would be an apology from the management. For many years the Belle's owner was a Mr. Prendergast who would apologise and ask people to be patient, saying that they were working as fast as they could to repair the fault.

Once or twice during the evening performance an usherette walked backwards down one aisle and up the other with a large metal contraption which emitted a perfumed spray to help freshen up the smoke laden air. The idea of the spray was good except if you were sitting in the seats near the aisle, as a fine shower of the perfumed disinfectant fell on you.

At the interval and sometimes during the films an usherette carried a tray which was supported with a strap around her neck. On the tray for sale were chocolates, ice cream and cigarettes. When the main film finished and the credits were rolling, just like the town centre cinemas, there was a rush to get out before the National Anthem.

One of the highlights of the week was the Saturday afternoon matinees, when children could go to the pictures for a halfpenny or a penny depending on where they sat or which cinema. I understand that you could get into the odd cinema for a jam jar, whether this is true or not I cannot say for sure. One thing I do remember was the noise, and it wasn't unusual for the cinema manager to stop the film and ask the children to be a little quieter.

Favourite films with the children were cowboys. Characters such as Tom Mix, Hoppalong Cassidy, Tonto, the Lone Ranger. Gene Autry, Roy Rogers and Trigger his horse. The cowboy pictures created a lot of excitement for the children, especially when the goodies were fighting the badies. There was great cheering when the goodies were winning, and plenty of booing,

152

when the badies seemed to have the upper hand carrying out their dirty deeds. Another favourite was Flash Gordon, who nearly every week got into a life threatening predicament just as the film was about to finish, leaving everyone on tenterhooks as to how Flash would get out of his near death problem. Then a voice would ask the question, "Was this the end for Flash Gordon? come next week to find out. Needless to say he always got out of his predicament.

The Keystone Cops, Laurel and Hardy and many other funny men helped to fill up the children's programme. Many times when the children were coming out after the show, they would enact some of the scenes that they had witnessed in the film shooting all and sundry with pretend guns.

The Belle use to put an advertisement in local church magazines and its motto was the clearest pictures in town, which was a little bit of an exaggeration as the films could have been well over a year old and well worn with use. Many is the time that there would be lines and white dots on the screen due to wear and tear.

Years ago the cinemas were not allowed to open on Sunday nights. Eventually the law changed but there were restrictions on opening times and films shown on Sundays. If I remember cinemas opened at four o'clock on Sunday afternoon and had to show a different film to the current programme. Also that some of the profit from the Sunday showing had to be given to charity.

Going to the cinema in the olden days, (as my grandchildren call them) was an enjoyable experience, with most of the films having happy endings. Although there were many weepy films as well but even most of these finished happily. One thing many of us enjoyed as we walked home, (maybe eating our fish and chips) was discussing the film's plot. It was like a bonus as many of us tried to rewrite the story with "what ifs". I'm sure you know what I mean if you lived in the olden days.

Our next port of call after going to the Belle in the evening was Grundy's "Fish and Chip" shop. It seemed part of the tradition after going to the pictures to call for fish and chips, many times we would ask for some scraps to put on our chips, scraps was cooked batter which had fallen off the fish. Chips and fish tasted really good eating them out of the bag as you walked home, especially on a cold evening. The shops of old did not carry the range of products like today; some of the chippies would have "turnovers" which were slices of potatoes cooked in batter, and also pies.

I recall that Grundy's chip range was coal fired. Mr. Grundy was a dab hand (forgive the pun) at feeding coal through the little opening into the fire and closing the fire door with quite a rattle. Later they had a gas range installed.

It is amazing how many fish and chip shops there were in the village. The ones I can remember were, four on Blackburn Road, one near the bridge, one near Penny Brow, one facing the Three Pigeons, (Grundy's) early in the 1930s one higher up than Isherwood and Fairclough's, one in Holly Street, Primula Street, Baxendale Street and two on Belmont Road one at the top of Ramsey Street, and one just below Bar lane.

Another thing I recall was customers taking their basins for their food and whilst they were waiting the shopkeeper would put their basin to warm on the chip range. Also people would take in newspapers which were used as a second wrap to keep the fish and chips warm. Obviously for health and safety reasons this isn't allowed today. Most of these have gone and have been replaced by other fast food outlets.

Next door to the Belle was a detached house in which lived a painter and decorator. We then come to the end of Hoyle Street, and on the south side is a row of six stone cottages, and the first one is a small grocers shop. At the other end The Gospel Hall, Maxwell Street.

THE GOSPEL HALL

The Brethren movement met at a number of places from 1854; however the church had grown so much that they purchased land and houses in Mayor Street where they built an Assembly known as the Hebron Hall. The new building opened on the 19th March 1910. A commerative booklet which celebrated 100 years of the Gospel Hall opening tells us that the new Hebron Hall had a number of members living in Astley Bridge and there was concern for the elderly having to travel so far especially in the cold winter months, so satellite meetings were held in Mr. and Mrs. Martins in Dormer Street.

In 1919 a small hall with kitchen and offices became vacant in Berkeley Road on land belonging to Heskeths mill. The Brethren members rented the property for 5/- per week.

Eventually a plot of land was bought in Maxwell Street and the building of the Gospel Hall was started. Although there is a date stone over the door showing 1938 the building was opened in the summer of 1939.

I remember as a child going to the hall on Saturday afternoon to children's meetings. There would be upwards of 50 children there, I cannot recall what the meetings were about, but am sure there would be a Christian message given to everyone there, however I do remember at the end of the meeting we were all given a glass of pop and some cake before going home.

HILLFOLD MILLS

Hill Fold Mills were built some time in the early 1860s. Samuel Hollins and his brother Frederick worked together under the title of Samuel Hollins and Co. However the partnership was dissolved 5th November 1863 and was reported in the London Gazette Co. 10th November 1863. The Company retained its original title. The Gazette refers to them as Cotton and Merino Spinners. I can only surmise that the spinning of wool was in the mills early days.

HILLFOLD MILLS

W A Openshaw took over the mill in 1900 that was until Joshua Barber & Co. Ltd acquired the business in 1916. Although the company traded under the Openshaw name their assets were taken over by Bolton Cotton Waste Co. a branch of Barber-Lomax.

Joshua Barber took under his wing his nephews Edward Pilkington Holden and Joshua Lomax. The latter took an additional forename of Barber, and in 1925 his descendants by deed poll hyphenated the two names as a surname Barber-Lomax. Bolton Cotton Waste (Holdings) Ltd changed its name to Barber Textile Corporation in 1946 then over a period of time took over other companies, and eventually being taken over by Spirella Ltd in 1971.

With the demise of the cotton industry in the county, shortly the take over Openshaw's closed down.

I can recall a conversation with my mother and some of her friends about working at Openshaw's when they were talking about the working conditions there; they said that the men working in the scutching hole (room) was probably one of the worst places to work in Bolton as Openshaw's worked waste cotton which was far from the best standards.

Another point about the mill was unlike all the other mills in Astley Bridge the owners did not appear to be involved in public affairs like other mill owners in the village.

After the war a number of pre-fab houses were built in the grounds of the mill to house workers from the Ukraine and other countries.

In 1974 the company "Indespension" moved from Holland Street and took over the Hill Fold factory for the manufacture of trailers. In 2000 the company moved to the Paragon Business Park in Horwich. (See page 104) Hill Fold Mills have been demolished and in its place is new housing development.

Moving further up Belmont Road we cross the old road to Blackburn at the top of Broad O'th Lane past a number of houses and arrive at IGW garage. Behind the garage and Arundel Street were a quarry and a brick works.

With the coming of the mills, houses were needed by the hundreds, however when the housing boom of the 1800s and early 1900s finished the brickworks closed down.

Between the Quarry and the Sweetloves Reservoir was a tennis club complete with a pavilion, long since gone, and above the club was Sweetloves reservoir.

SWEETLOVES RESERVOIR

Sweetloves gets its name from a farm named after Edmund
Sweetlove who took a lease in 1712. In 1824 Sweetloves
Reservoir was built on the site to take water from local springs.

Built in 1824
Extended in 1863
Catchment area 43 acres
Average Rainfall 55 inches
Top of water above sea level 517 feet
Area of water 12.66 Acres
Total capacity 80 million gallons
Maximum depth 36 feet
Length of dam 601 feet
Height of dam, 43 feet 6 inches.

The reservoir was drained sometime before the long hot summer
of 1996 for housing development by Barratt's, and also Jones
building companies.
On the northern side of the development is Wilkinson Road,
behind which is North Bolton Ambulance Station, followed by
Shoreswood where more post war building can be seen. There is
a stone boundary wall on the north of Shoreswood which
marked the southern boundary of the Wilkinson estate. By the
wall is an ancient foot path leading to Barrow Bridge, It goes
past Oldhams estate through to Tippet House, across Smithills
Dean Road, behind Sheep House farm and down over a bridge
to where the wooden tea rooms stood at the side of the lake.
Sadly the lake is no more, it has gone the way of many things
and is now a car park.

WILKINSON'S SANITORIAM

As we progress up Belmont Road we pass a new private housing estate which was built on the land where Whitehill House used to stand. The house was built by Thomas Wilkinson in 1868 in 8 acres of ground. Journal and Guardian 14th November 1935 reports that he started work probably part time aged 8 at Slater's Croft, however he after two years he went to Bolton Grammar School. He was quite athletic at school. He became a cobbler's assistant at 3/- per week. He moved on from there to work for Mr James Haslam a cotton waste dealer.

One of his jobs was to clean his master's boots each morning something to which he objected, and one morning filled the boots with blacking as a protest.

After 10 years he set up business on his own with the princely sum of £10. In the beginning times were hard as he had a wife and home to keep. He battled on and money started to pour into the coffers.

He became a councillor as a Radical and led a crusade against cellar dwellings, which were shameful, unsanitary and terrible slums. He worked diligently for the cellar dwellers, and the majority of these terrible slums were done away with.

In 1907 he announced at a dinner party that he was giving his house "Whitehill" to the town to be used as a sanatorium for consumption, or as it was known by many as the Great white plague, He also gave an endowment of £50,000 towards its upkeep, together with the house and grounds the gift was worth around £100,000.

T. B was rife amongst many cotton workers, fresh air and good food were used in the fight against T B. Sufferers could be in the sanatorium for months and there were many deaths, which rather unfairly gave the sanatorium the name of "The death house" but by 1915 the sanatorium, together with action on overcrowding in living conditions, and malnutrition the health of the town was getting better.

By the 1960s T B had been virtually beaten and the sanatorium became a convalescent home. Eventually the place closed completely in 1979.

WILKINSON'S SANATORIUM, BOLTON.

THOMAS WILKINSON

Born 1926
Married
Freeman of Bolton 6th November 1910
Philanthropist
Died 26th December 1916
Buried Egerton U R C churchyard

Whitehill House has been demolished and replaced with a new housing estate.
Whitehill Cottages originally called Long Row are still there, and it was in one of these cottages that Methodism took root in Astley Bridge. These eight cottages are one of the gems of

Astley Bridge with lovely hanging baskets at the side of their doors and beautiful gardens at the front. Probably the best known house in the row is the "Top Shop". It is on the Belmont Road end of the cottages, a little oasis in an area where shops are few or even

none existent where locals can top up their larders with groceries fruit and vegetables, and tasty ice cream.

Whitehill cottages are some of the oldest in Astley Bridge being built in the early 1800s. The majority of the stone cottages and houses throughout the area were built up to and around 1850.

HORROCKS FOLD AND MOOR

Horrocks Fold is a little hamlet just off Belmont Road. There is a grade 2 listed 15th century farmhouse standing in four acres of land which has been updated, and further development turning the barn into a home and other new houses built. The Fold stands on the edge of Horrocks Moor.

A windswept area of moorland, part of which, if not most, is managed by the Forestry Commission. Here again like Horrocks Fold we have another farm, Horrocks Hill Farm which has been redeveloped with modern home accommodation.

As we travel further up Belmont Road from Horrocks Fold we pass quite a number of well cared for semi and detached houses, with immaculate gardens. These houses have wonderful views looking to the east over Egerton with its famous Egerton Mills which is now partly an industrial estate, and the Darwen Moors, Turton Heights.

Nestling in the moorland about up to half a mile from the nearest building is the Wilton Arms which is quite a popular venue. Prior to becoming a restaurant, it was a country public house complete with a very tricky bowling green. The green fell away greatly on one side, making it difficult to keep ones bowls on the green. It has now been made into an extra car park.

Horrocks Moor covers quite a fair area, and within its boundaries lies some of Whimberry Hill, which is a place which lived up to its name certainly in the 1930s, 40s, and 50s. There would be scores of people armed with boxes and bowls gathering whimberries, this was before the coming of the plastic bag. In fact for many people it was a day out, there, people were enjoying the fresh, clean country air, free from the smoke and grime of the mills and houses. It was a family occasion, not only to pick fruit but also have a picnic, and for the younger people a roly poly down the hillside.

PART OF HORROCKS MOOR WITH THE WILTON ARMS IN THE DISTANCE

There is a large man made forest on the moor. On 1st September 1919 the Forestry Act came into force. After the First World War, especially through trench warfare our timber stocks were so depleted that something urgent had to be done. The first forestry commission trees were planted 8th December 1919. The trees on the moor were planted in the late 20s and early 30s. On the moor are the 4 Wilton Quarries from which grit sandstone was produced mainly for building and flagging. The 1885 Directory show them as owned by Wood and Warburton. The quarries closed some time around the Second World War. Although the quarries are now defunct for quarrying stone they are well used recreation areas.

Wilton 1 is owned by the BMC for the benefit of climbers and you can climb here at any time.

Wilton 2, 3 and 4 are owned by the resident shooting club with agreed times for shooting and climbing - live firing takes place and it is vital that climbers understand and stick to the following arrangements. The access arrangements are as follows:

Wilton 2 & 4: Climbers have priority on Tuesdays, Thursdays and Saturdays.

Wilton 3: Climbers have priority on Mondays, Tuesdays, Thursdays and Saturdays.

On days when shooters have priority (and the red warning flags are not in place), climbers can access the quarries for climbing, but they *should leave at the shooters request. Please try to avoid* the temptation of assuming that the ranges are not being used until at least mid-afternoon.

On days when climbers have priority, the shooters can use the sites if climbers are not present when they arrive. However, if climbers arrive, shooting must cease. Please allow them a reasonable time to clear up.

If, the shooters are using Wilton 2, but are not in Wilton 3, climbers can still use Wilton 3, provided that they do not climb the routes on Orange Wall (i.e. routes between Twin Cracks and Orange Corner inclusive). Climbers must then not pass the fence on the ridge between Wilton 2 and 3 or descend past it.

The Wilton Quarries, just North of Bolton, are the most important rock climbing site in Lancashire and the North West, with well over 400 climbs, representing over 12% of the routes within the Lancashire Area. Not only does Wilton contain a large proportion of the climbs in Lancashire, but these climbs span all the grades and represent the very finest of quarry climbs. These and many others are truly classic climbs that have provided sport and enjoyment for nearly fifty years – A recreational resource that is central to Lancashire climbing, and which has been the starting point for a lifetime on the crags for countless climbers from the surrounding mill towns.

Thus, climbers were very concerned when United Utilities decided to put all the Wilton Quarries up for sale by auction, which could have meant the loss of this valuable recreational amenity. The British Mountaineering Council has today purchased the largest of the Wilton Quarries, and has negotiated permanent access arrangements with Bolton Rifle and Pistol Club, who are purchasing the other quarries.

Wilton 1 is the largest with probably the most interesting rock form, known as the "Prow" The quarries are a great attraction to climbers, although Bolton Gun Club uses Wilton 2 & 3 on certain days of the week. When the gun club are active they fly a red flag at the entrance to the quarry. Incidentally the current joining fee for the club is £15 and a £350 per annum subscription. Bird watchers are also found around the quarries with many species of birds being spotted. Walking groups and ramblers make the quarries one of their focal points on their moorland walks.

HURRICANE FIGHTER

On the 2nd February 1945 two Hurricanes took off for a training flight from RAF Calverly in Cheshire, whilst they flew in formation unfortunately they collided in some cloud and crashed on Whimberry Hill. The plane exploded on impact and was completely destroyed. The pilot Flight Sergeant Thomas Stanley Taylor was killed. The other plane crashed some ¾ mile away.

Through Horrocks Moor runs Scout Road probably one of the most dangerous roads for accidents in the town. Whilst most of the road is straight with good visibility there are two very dangerous bends one about 400 yards from Belmont Road and another at the Walker Fold end. The bend near Belmont Road has had a number of accidents, some with fatalities.

The most recent was Thursday 31st May 2012 when a Mercedes car plunged over the cliff edge crashing through the barrier and rolling over a number of times taking with it some of the safety barrier. The man suffered serious injuries to his head and back. He was taken to Salford Royal Hospital.

In June 2010 a red Peugeot crashed near the same spot at 10-30 pm. It tumbled over the cliff edge; the 44 year old driver was taken to Royal Bolton Hospital with minor injuries to his head and back.

A few years earlier, two brothers were approaching the notorious bend when suddenly the car seemed to go out of control and went over the edge of the cliff dropping some 300 yards before stopping on its roof. One of the brothers got out unharmed but the other was taken to hospital.

The Forestry Commission built a car park on the moor, they chose a really wonderful spot with uninterrupted views overlooking Bolton, Salford and Manchester to the south and Wigan and other towns to the west.

From this point you can see in the distance the Derbyshire hills, Jodrell Bank, and many other places from Cheshire to North Wales. During the celebration of Queen Elizabeth's Diamond Jubilee celebrations a beacon was lit near the car park.

The last property we come too in Astley Bridge going up Belmont Road is the Wilton Arms Restaurant. Many years ago the Wilton was a country pub and had a very tricky crown bowling green, with one part of the green falling away quite a lot, this made it quite difficult to keep the bowls on the green. The green is now a car park.

Having passed the Wilton Arms we soon come to the Astley Bridge boundary with Blackburn, returning our way down Belmont Road the view across to Egerton is quite peaceful. There is also a top class hotel in Egerton village well known for friendliness, quality and service.

EGERTON HOUSE

Whilst Egerton House is not in Astley Bridge it has strong connections with the village. It was initially a farm. Just the centre of the house is original, and the barn is the only other building left of the old farm. It once belonged to the cotton spinners Ashworths, after that the bleaching family of the Deakins became the owners. A son of the Ashworths married a daughter of the Deakins and they lived there from 1902 until the early 60s.

Edmund Ashworth's ashes are buried in the grounds.

In 1971 it was converted into a Country House Hotel, eventually it was bought by MacDonald Hotels who on the 18th December sold it to Jan Hampton whose skills and drive have more than established Egerton House as one of the best in the traditional county of Lancashire.

EGERTON HOUSE

As we make our way back from the boundary, on our left is Gale farm, and the village of Egerton.

Gleaves Reservoir is in the foreground. It is triangular in shape and just after the war a model boat club used the reservoir regularly, unfortunately there was a lot of vandalism to their hut and facilities, so much so I believe that the venue was abandoned. It is now one of Bolton & District Anglers Associations waters.

Just a short walk south from Gleaves reservoir was Springfield Bleachworks which was taken over by Wolstenhome Bronze Powders when the bleachworks closed. Wolstenhomes unfortunately went in to liquidation and the whole site has been taken for housing. The factory has gone and the lodge which was firstly a quarry has been filled in.

On 2nd February 1943 my friends and I were sitting on the horse trough at the junction of Belmont Road and Blackburn Road when we heard a plane which sounded in trouble, its engine was spluttering and the plane appeared to be losing height. We watched the plane until it went out of sight, but we did hear its engine fail.

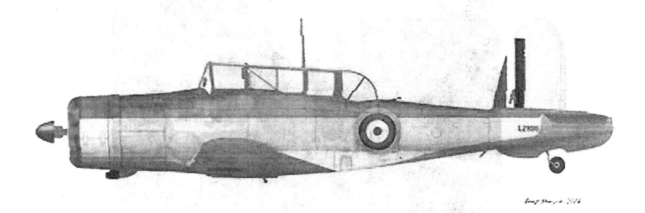

The plane turned out to be a Blackburn Skua L 2892 of 776 Squadron flying from RAF Woodvale to Speke. The plane attempted to land in a field just south of the quarry lodge, but unfortunately it skidded for about 100 yards be fore hitting a wall turned over and finished up in the lodge. The plane sank immediately, both crew members were killed. The recovery team arrived the next day. The salvage operation was quite difficult due not only to the land being quite boggy. The team were unable to get crane near but also the plane was in 60 feet of water. Eventually the plane was recovered with a hauser.

The engine was too deeply embedded in the mud for the divers to retrieve, and it lay there until Bolton sub-aqua club successfully recovered the engine in 1974. It was cleaned and given to the RAF Museum at Cardington.

The two crew members were Sub Lt A J Newton and air gunner A/s L Maiston. A few days later we went to look at the site where the accident had happened and found an area where the plane had landed, and it had left a gouged track of land up to about 100 yards long by 6 to 8 feet wide and roughly 12 inches to 18 inches deep.

From the boundary with Blackburn to Templecombe Drive is probably the longest piece of road in Astley Bridge without a building being alongside the road. On this stretch, is what was one of the most dangerous bends in the area. Vehicles, mainly motor cycles coming down from Belmont past the Wilton would hit the bend and lose control leaving the road and crash down into the field. Some years after the war, alterations were made with crash barriers and dangerous bend warnings being installed.

There is a vast expanse of land between the road and Egerton, and whilst there is still a lot of farmland and woodland a tremendous amount of private house building has gone on since the war. Just north of Templecomb Drive was a reservoir which was filled in after the last war. It was built before 1850 and probably belonged to Springfield bleachworks, although I have no proof of this. It is shown on old maps, but now is just grassland. Whether it was just a fisherman's tale or not I cannot say, but local fishermen said that it was teaming with fish and yet the owner whoever that was would not allow people to fish in this reservoir.

Just south of Eagley Brook and Egerton Mills runs Longworth Road which straddles Dunscar Golf Course. The club was founded in 1908. The course is in a beautiful area of moorland with heather and gorse here and there, and a breathtaking view of higher moorland around. Being a moorland course I am sure that it can get a little windy at times but after playing a round of golf you may feel tired but also invigorated.

Continuing down Belmont Road was Ingledene Nursing Home. I do not know what happened to the home or when it closed and now we now pass more post war houses to Whitehill Lane where there used to be a very popular restaurant called "Summerhills", which was a favourite for Christmas Parties and special occasions.

Close by, is what was Bolton Corporation Waterworks Sweetloves Water Treatment Plant. In 1824 a company was set up called The Company of Proprietors of Greater and Little Bolton Waterworks, especially to develop water supplies in the Bolton area. On 29th September the waterworks were purchased by the council, thus becoming Bolton Corporation Waterworks. The waterworks grew in size by amalgamating with other waterworks, and by 1950 Bolton was responsible for supplying water to 470 thousand people. Bolton got its water from gathering grounds in the local surrounding moorland areas, also from wells. The filter bed plant was built in 1886 and as of now takes water from Dingle, Springs, Delph and Entwistle reservoirs, quite a cocktail. One interesting fact is that the water from Entwistle reservoir relies purely on gravity to get to Sweetloves, there are no pumps involved in the project. Google say that Entwistle is about 215 Metres above sea level whilst Sweetloves is around 177 metres

SWEETLOVES WATERWORKS BUILDING

BOLTON WATERWORKS MOTTIVE ON WALL AND COTTAGE AT SPRINGS

Springs is the earliest being built in 1830, named after the spring from Daddies Meadows which feeds the reservoir.

Entwistle built 1837 which is a little unusual for two reasons. 1-- It was first used to control river flow for the benefit of the bleachworks (compensation water). Secondly it had the first earth dam of over a hundred feet in the country. Its dam was raised in 1840 to give more capacity.

Dingle built in 1850 named after the area Shaley Dingle.

And finally Delph built in 1921 although considered for construction in 1853. Building started in 1909 but due to the First World War was not finished until 1921.

It was recognise that more water would be needed with Manchester looking at the possibility of bringing water from the Lake District. The cost of building an aqueduct around a hundred miles long was very daunting; however Bolton together with possibly other Authorities shared some of the cost. This was great fete of engineering as the water flows through the aqueduct by the force of gravity for around ninety-six miles. The project was completed in stages, and on 7th January 1942. Bolton started to draw water from Thirlmere in the Lake District.

In 1987 the water industry was privatised and Northwest Water took over the operation. At the time of takeover the Bolton waterworks department employed about 400 people.

In 1847 the demand for 100 thousand people was 1.4 million gallons and by the 1980s it had risen to 5.3 million gallons. In 1995 North West water Authority merged with Norweb becoming United Utilities.

Sweetloves treatment works supplies pure and clean drinking water for most of the homes on the north side of Bolton.

The water treatment plant is fully automated and on an open day some years ago we were told that during the week just 4 people run the plant, however at week end it is run automatically but not to worry if something went wrong people could be there in a very short time.

On Wednesday 5th September 2012 a major problem arose. Belmont Road had to be closed because the 24 inch pipe bringing water from Delph reservoir bursted causing horrendous chaos to traffic because Belmont Road had to be closed.

As we come down Belmont Road we come somewhere near High Houses. I am not sure if the original houses are still standing. The only reference which I have come across so far is the following report of the Medical Officer of Health on the condition of High Houses was read.

To the Chairman of Astley Bridge Local Board—17th May 1876.

Sir,

At your request I have visited High Houses. The tenants at numbers 5 & 6 complained some months ago of imperfect drainage, which has since been rectified, though the nuisance arising from non-trapping of the pipe remains. There is neither privy or ashpit for these houses, and the tenants complain greatly of the want of them. At Walsh's farmhouse there is a large hole within a short distance from the door, into which the refuse water of the house runs; a proper drain and grid are required, which can be easily supplies at a small expense. The imperfect drainage complained of by Messrs Ferguson and Dowling has been attended to, the drain having been re-laid. I am very truly, R Settle Medical Officer of Health. The attention of the owners of the property was directed to be called to the matter on the motion of Mr Liptrott and seconded by Mr Cooper.

Next comes High View House which is now a Kindergarten. Just before we arrive at Sweetloves Lane, we come to some Playing fields belonging to High Lawn Primary School.

HIGH LAWN

High Lawn, Sharples the Residence of J.A. Slater Esq., 1886

by John Bradshaw Gass (1855-1939)

HIGH LAWN · SHARPLES · · THE RESIDENCE OF J.A. SLATER ESQ

The fields and the land which the school stands on were
originally part of the High Lawn estate.
The architect of High Lawn House was John Bradshaw Gass.
It was quite a handsome mansion, south facing with 4 reasonable
sized entertaining rooms, 8 bedrooms and several changing
rooms, the house was furnished with furniture only of the best
quality. The gardens were well designed with bushes along
each side of the drive which was some 300 yards long with a
gate house at the entrance. 2 massive gate posts supported
the large iron gates. There was a kitchen garden, hot
houses and tennis courts. At the north of the building were
stables and a coach house. John Magnall was the owner

JOHN MAGNALL

Born about 1781
A member of the Bolton Light Horse Volunteers
Purchased Springfield paper mills between 1834 and 1836
John ran the mills with his 2 sons Walter and Wilbraham.
Died 1865
Another owner of High lawn was J A Slater Esq. who lived
there around 1886
William Tristram owner of Peakes mill in Halliwell which
became Burtons clothing factory was another person who
bought High Lawn, but unfortunately no dates.
The house was demolished some time before the last war, and
the land lay derelict for a number of years. A piece of the land
bordering Sweetloves Lane and Belmont Road was used as a
football pitch for a number of years. We played on this land
many times using coats as goal posts.
In the early 1950s the land was developed for a new primary
school and High lawn school opened in 1954.

As we progress further down Belmont Road we pass a mixture
of nice looking houses and bungalows built I believe some time
in the early 1930s, we pass Wilmslow and Alderley Avenues,
and arrive at Douglas Street coming to our fourth Co-operative
store, Built in 1900. We pass a short row of houses, and then
crossing Bar Lane to the next row of buildings which is or was a
mixture of dwelling houses and shops. I recall a greengrocers, a
bakers, a grocers, and a chip shop in this row.
Now we cross Westminster Road, more houses, until we come
to what was the Carters Arms now called the Tap which is
owned by the local Bank Top Brewery.
Crossing Ramsey Street we approach another chip shop at the
top of Pemberton Street and other dwellings including the
British Legion, which I believe is, or was celebrating its 80th
birthday in Astley Bridge.

Passing Lawson Street there was a row of houses down to the Three Pigeons public House. These were demolished for road improvements.

Before major road improvements, which included ash felting, the roads and also the pavements down to the road junction and on the Blackburn Road side together with the small car park in front of the Three Pigeons all these areas were cobbled. There was also a horse trough at the junction which was kindly donated by Misses Wolfenden in June 1896. By 1939 the trough had become redundant and the water supply was disconnected and also all the troughs water fittings were taken away. Looking at old photographs before alterations to the road junction the trough was right on the edge of the road.

The trough was a favourite place for young people to meet and pass the time of day, and it wasn't unusual to see up to half a dozen young people from about 11 to 14 years old sitting on the trough.

In 1952 the council decided to remove the trough, and they put it somewhere on a grassy bank near Harricroft farm. However a number of local Astley Bridge lads felt that this decision wasn't quite the thing. One of the lads borrowed his uncles vehicle, which they would use to carry the trough back to its rightful place (in their eyes) but unfortunately it was so heavy that fell off the vehicle. It was general knowledge that the local Astley Bridge based in the old Police Station on Blackburn Road knew who the culprits were, but decided that the lads would get into serious trouble with the boys uncle, so they took no action.

In those days Bolton Had its own Chief Constable who had decided that people responsible should be brought to justice. The case was reported in the Bolton Evening News with the headline THE VIGILANTES OF ASTLEY BRIDGE.

Just behind the trough was a very handsome lamp standard standing on a circle of stone. Also there was and still is a telephone booth. Way back 50 years or so and in the days of old imperial money, it cost old pennies to make a phone call, also very few people had a telephone and there was a waiting list for installations. Even when you got to the top of the list you may have to share a line with someone else, which could be very inconvenient should you want to make an urgent call as they could be using the line.

So going back to those days public call boxes were well used, and the one near the horse trough was quite busy at times with thre or four people queuing to use the 'phone.

To use the 'phone you had to insert two pennies into a slot in a big black metal box on which the 'phone was fixed, and in the 1930s you picked up the 'phone and you spoke to an operator giving the telephone number you required as there was no self dialling in those days.

During the day they were female operators and in the evening the males took over. On the black box were two buttons marked

A and B, the operator would put you through to the required number and you would hear it ringing as soon as you heard someone answer you had to press button A, you would then hear the pennies drop and when this happened you were connected. If there was no answer you would in this case, press button B and your money was returned.

I am sure that there were a lot of lads who would just go into the call box and press button B perchance someone who had used the 'phone earlier and could not get through forgetting to get their money back.

THE THREE PIGEONS

This building is quite a landmark in the village, and in its time not only is it one of the oldest inns in Astley Bridge but has been one of the best supported. Before the war the small car park at the front was a favourite meeting place for cycle club outings. There was a Jug and Bottle department entrance on Belmont Road corner of the building which was squared up and bricked up many years ago.

On the Blackburn Road side there was an entrance to a cellar workshop, which was rented out and used by a local plumber

Robert Scholes as was the a large wooden garage next door which opened onto Blackburn Road. The garage caught fire around 1941 but the fire was soon under control. The garage and other buildings were demolished some time after the war to make way for some extensions which made the building around double in size. Also a portico was built at the front.

When the houses at the rear of the inn both on Belmont and Blackburn Roads were taken down a car park was built in their place. Threlfalls was the beer that the Three Pigeons sold for many years. In winter they brewed a stronger beer called Falstaff.

The road layouts were changed around the 1950s-60s Belmont Road was made one way from the Blackburn Road junction to Lawson Street. A one way system was then made one from Belmont Road down Lawson Street to Blackburn Road.

The Farnworth journal dated Saturday 20th May 1876 reported that Nathan Kay and Son of Horrocks Fold applied to erect a slaughter house near Belmont Road, I wonder if it is the one in Lawson Street, it wasn't very big holding only a handful of cattle at a time. To get to the abattoir the animals were herded through the back yards of the two shops namely Myers Newsagents and Higson's Greengrocers which were between Lawson Street and Back Blackburn Road. Eventually the slaughter house closed, and a Painter and Decorator, Mr Granville Bullough took it over as a workshop.

I remember as a lad, we would sit on a book on a roller skate and trundle down the steep incline of the backstreet between the greengrocers and Birchall's butchers to the road. On reflection this was quite dangerous as there were times when you could lose control and finish up on the road, but in those wartime days there was very little traffic.

Astley Bridge Post Office was on the corner of Pemberton Street, it was also a grocers shop owned by Fred Brown who ran the business for many years until his daughter Dylis took over. After some years probably with the arrival of Asda the grocery side ended and now it is just a post office which also stocks stationary.

As we progress up Blackburn Road passing Ramsay Street, and Westminster Road. The next row of houses is a mixture of red brick and stone, both large and small. In this row is an ironmonger's come DIY shop, which trades as the "Homecare Centre". This shop is like Aladdin's cave, filled to the gunnels with nearly everything one needs for home improvement. This is probably one of the oldest shops in the village and has been of service as long as I can remember.

At number 711 lived Astley Bridges most famous son Arthur Henry Rostron.

ARTHUR HENRY ROSTRON

Born 4th May 1869

Baptised 19th June 1869 by Rev Birley of St Pauls Astley Bridge

Married to Ethel Minnie Stothert 14th September 1899, at St John the Baptist Atherton. Her father was Richard Stothert

RICHARD STOTHERT

Richard Stothert arrived in Atherton in the 1850s from the Preston area of Lancashire, Goosnargh to be precise. He founded a small pills & potions drug manufactory including medicants such as zinc ointment and boracic acid. The factory was at Albion House in the Bag Lane area of Atherton. The business prospered and in the 20th century ventured into pop manufacture (sweet, aerated, sugar-filled mineral waters) - Tizer was a favourite orange flavoured tooth-rotter (I drank gallons of Tizer as a kid, and now have a mouth full of heavy/noble metals). In the 1960-70s Stotherts were absorbed by Barrs of Glasgow, and Stotherts of Atherton is now one of their 4 main canning plants. They make a product called IRN-BRU, the drinking of which is like sucking on a sugar coated rusty nail that's been rubbed in an ash tray, then stuck into a tangerine. Hyperactivity guaranteed. Written by Peter Wood.

These two pages were missing when Norman left us, but I presume he intended it to be about the Astley Bridge connection to the Sinking of the Titanic, I feel it would be wrong for me to add my version, so I leave it to the reader to research as Norman would have done. AR.

Whilst, quite rightly Arthur Rostron was a hero, it was another Bolton man was probably unfairly made out to be a villain, and that man was Captain Stanley Lord.

Captain Stanley Lord
Born13th September 1877
Lived in Hampden Street Bolton
Married Mabel Tutton 19th March 1907 at St Mary's, Walton Liverpool.
One son Stanley Tutton Lord born15th August 1908, died 1st December 1994

I feel that captain Lord was made a scapegoat for other people's inadequacies. Captain Lord always protested his innocence.

His radio operator switched off the radio at 11-15 pm and went to bed. Later rockets were seen and Captain Lord was informed, he said that he thought there was a party on board, and we must not forget that it was claimed that the Titanic was unsinkable.

The inquiries concluded that the Californian had indeed been just six miles to the north of Titanic and could have reached the Titanic before it sank, but was it the Californian?

His ship was proved farther away from the disaster than the authorities claimed.
Some questions and during the various enquiries were raised.

Captain E J Smith of the Titanic ignored seven ice berg warnings from his crew and other ships.
The 16 watertight compartments were not as high as they should have been because more room was needed for passengers, had they been higher it is possible the ship would not have sunk.
There were not enough lifeboats.
It was believed that the Managing Director of WHITE Star Line, Mr Bruce Ismay put pressure on Captain Smith to maintain the speed of the ship for propaganda purposes.

On 1st September 1985 a French/American team found the wreck of the Titanic at a depth just under two and a half miles down, with debris strewn over a 15 square mile area. When some of the rivets were recovered, a number of them were found to be made from a sub-standard iron.

Any reasons Captain Lord gave were brushed aside, some of his evidence was ignored. The Titanic was claimed to be virtually unsinkable which proved not to be the case. I feel that had the Californian not have been in the area, other heads would have rolled. It was very convenient for authorities on both sides of the Atlantic to condemn Captain Lord to cover up many things that went wrong on that fateful Sunday night on 13th April 1912.

As we have covered the next 3 to 400 yards earlier we now move up Blackburn Road towards Sweetloves Lane where there was many years ago a large sand pit, and also nearby a coal pit. Next is Holden Avenue which together with Sharples, Eastgrove and Southgrove Avenues is built on possibly the hilliest parts of Astley Bridge. It is an attractive estate of mainly semi detached pre war houses. It is here on Sharples Avenue where we find our fifth Co-op store. Going north past Stavely Avenue we find one of only two petrol stations in Astley Bridge, the other is at Asda. Next is a newish post war housing development. I remember that this area was a cow meadow. Unfortunately it used to get quite waterlogged and the first building to go on the land I understand had a lot of problems with water. On the corner of Kermoor Avenue is the Mandalay Health Centre, it is quite secluded and unobtrusive, in fact as you pass by the building does it not give the impression of being a busy Medical Centre with around seven doctors and many ancillary medical and non medical staff. At the rear is quite large car park.

We move on past Kermoor Avenue to Springfield Road, along this road on the right was an old gravel pit in operation in the 1800s. Here again more houses were built after the war. Back on Blackburn Road we come to a row of stone buildings which include what was the Cheetham Arms now the Brewhouse. It is and inn and restaurant which was refurbished in 2009. There are four en-suite bedrooms. In the tramways early days, the terminus from Bolton was outside the Cheetham Arms. The line from the Cheetham to Dunscar Bridge was completed later when funds were available. On the journey to wards Longworth Lane we pass a number of houses which are a lot higher than the road. Some time after the war, one of the residents decided to dig out some of the hillside below his house, but before he could build a strong retaining wall we had some atrocious weather and there was a great possibility of a land slip. The whole project was shored up for many months, until a substantial concrete wall was built.

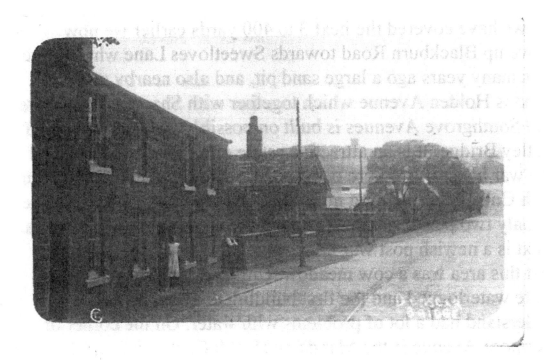

COTTAGES ON BLACKBURN ROAD WHO'S HOUSE DOOR NUMBERS ARE OVER 1,000

Passing a short row of houses with house whose door numbers are over 1,000. We have now arrived at the Dunscar Bridge boundary which crosses Eagley Brook, where I understand from local fishermen contains trout.

The old Dunscar bus terminus is now a little derelict as it is no longer used as bus turn round, and is used as a car park and at times a vegetable stall has stood there. When the trams were running the bridge was the terminus. Here the tram stopped and the driver climbed down from the platform went to a nearby lamp post to where a long trolley pole was fastened, he took the pole and attached it to the trolley which drew electricity from the over power line. He then pulled the trolley down off the wire, pulled it to the other end of the tram and reconnected the trolley to the line ready for the return journey. He then replaced the pole on to the lamp post.

Whilst the driver was engaged changing the trolley, the conductor would be pushing the backs of the seats, forward to face the opposite way so when passengers got on board they would be facing the way the tram was going. In the thirties and forties every tram or bus had both a driver and conductor. Whilst the driver was in charge of the tram overall, the conductors job was to collect the fares and issue tickets. Their were tickets of different values depending on the length of your journey and also if you were a child. All these various tickets were attached to a piece of wooden board, the conductor would take the relevant ticket for the journey and on a belt he had a clipping machine and he would clip the ticket at the stage where you got on the vehicle. All the fare he put into a leather bag which was strapped over his or her shoulder. The conductor was also responsible for ringing the bell by pulling on a wire which went down the length of the tram. This alerted the driver of a passenger wishing to get off at the next stop and also when it *was safe to start the tram after all the passengers had boarded.* When the conductor had quiet moment he or she would start to count all the coppers which they had taken. They would count out 60 pennies then roll them into a piece of paper making a tube they would then tuck the ends of the tube, they would do the same with all the halfpennies, so they had 5/- rolls of pennies and 2/6 rolls of halfpennies ready to pay in at the office.

Our return journey from Dunscar Bridge takes us past Shore Lodge which is very popular with anglers with over half a dozen fishing lodge called Atkinson Reservoir. Between the reservoir and Blackburn Road was a large sand pit which nature has reclaimed. As we approach the corner of Eagley way we find a Lodge house, at the rear is the Eagley Bowling Club which was built over 150 years ago for the benefit of the managers at Eagley mills. It is now a private club but still owned by the mills owners. The members pay a peppercorn rent for the facility. In 2009 the green plus Atkinson Reservoir were put on the market. The green for £20,000, and fishing rights both to the reservoir and Eagley Brook from £10,000 to £25,000. However there have been no takers much to the relief of the Eagley bowlers.

188

In March 1999. The clubhouse was attacked by vandals who ripped off window shutters broke the windows throwing glass and other debris onto the green. The toilets were wrecked. They damaged virtually everything in the clubhouse and sprayed graffiti all over the place. A night-watchman lived in the gatehouse which is on the corner of Eagley Way. As we crossover the Way we come to the entrance to Makants farm which leads to Park View and Terrace.

ANOTHER GEM OF ASTLEY BRIDGE PARK VIEW

Continuing down Blackburn Road we come to where the Eagley Sunday School Social Club "Westcliffe" was situated, which for many years had a couple of tennis courts on the corner of Westcliffe Road and Blackburn Road, finally down to Northland Road and Andrew Lane. Having past Holden's mill we make our way to Ashworth Lane one of the oldest minor roads in Astley Bridge. In the 1940s Dr Frank's surgery stood on one corner and on the other a sweet shop with a temperance bar. In its early days it was known as Ashworths Lane (the lane going to Ashworths mill).

There is a mixture of terraced houses on one side and semi-detached on the other, where we find the sixth Co-op shop in the village. Most of the houses on this side of the lane from the Co-op to the row of red brick terrace were built between the wars. However just before the red brick terrace was Hill Cot House at one time the home of Sir John Holden and his wife. The Holden's then moved to "The Firs" in Leigh. Eventually Sir John and his wife went to live at Ollerton Hall whilst George moved into "The Firs" at Leigh.

Hill Cot had a very long garden and in the garden were a number of apple trees which were quite tempting when in fruit. There was just a low wall separating people from the orchard, which meant it was easy to nip into the garden and pinch an apple. The only thing was the apples were not eaters but bakers and they played havoc with your stomach.

The house now is part of Sharples Secondary School which opened in 1975. It is now known as Sharples Science College with a school motto of "Preparing for Success" Since being built the school has undergone a number of changes and extensions. The College is also known as the Sharples Community Leisure Centre containing a sports hall, swimming pool, gym, squash courts, and 2 all weather pitches, which are quite an asset to local people.

We are now coming to one of the oldest parts of Astley Bridge, the village of Bank Top. This village came about because of the Ashworth family. Nearby is Sharples Primary School which opened in 1969 replacing the old stone built school in the centre of Bank Top village. The new school is at the top of Hugh Lupos Street.

ASHWORTHS

The Ashworth family came to Bolton in 1665 to escape the great plague which was rampant in London. Plague wasn't new to England although the 1665 sickness was the worst ever. Many areas of London in those days were poverty stricken and full of squalor, rubbish and all kinds of waste including human was just thrown into the streets. The place was filthy and a breeding ground for disease. Lots of people thought that the plague was being carried by cats and dogs and many were destroyed. In fact the disease was carried by fleas which lived on rats. Where a family or household had the disease they had to paint a red cross on the door to warn people. At the time there was a great exodus from London with hundreds and hundreds of people moving out into the country. Many people will remember the children's skipping song which referred to the plague.

"Ring a ring of roses, a pocket full of posies
Attishoo, attishoo we all fall down."

The first part refers to the red circular blotches which were found on the skin which developed into large pus filled sacs and were very painful. The second part refers to the belief that the disease was spread by a cloud of poisonous gas germs, and by carrying a posy it would overpower the germs. Finally a sneezing fit was followed by death. One tragedy at the time which probably became a blessing was the great fire of London, which started in a small way in the bakeshop of Thomas Farynor baker to King Charles II in Pudding Lane at one o'clock in the morning on 2nd September 1666. At this time most of the houses were made of wood and pitch which were very inflammable. A very high wind fanned the flames; in fact the fire would have done more damage had it not been for a previous bad fire in 1633 which had created a gap in the buildings. The amazing thing was that although the fire covered about 430 acres, which represented 80% destroying some 13,000 houses, 89 churches and 52 guild halls making thousands of people homeless and financially ruined it is believed that less than 20 people perished. The blessing if you can call it that was that the plague diminished, probably due to all the plague carrying rats which were killed in the blaze.

On arrival in Bolton the Ashworths bought a farm and land at Birtenshaw. The coming of their family would change the face of Astley Bridge from being an area of farms, fields and cottage industries into part of the industrial revolution which was sweeping the country in the 18th and 19th century.

John Ashworth was born in 1696 and was instrumental in starting the great cotton empire of the Ashworth family. In his early days he bought the raw cotton from Liverpool and sold or loaned the cotton to the local cottage cotton spinners, buying the spun cotton from them, and using the same principles he passed the cotton to the cottage weavers again paying them for the finished cloth.

The Ashworths were a Quaker family. It is recorded that the first Quaker meeting in Bolton was 1668 probably led by Mr James Harrison. In 1672 Phineas Pemberton came to Bolton and married James daughter Pheobe. The two families held Quaker meetings at the Harrison home, and some time later James was arrested for preaching to the people that they should "repent and fear God not man and seek the way of light and truth". For this he was fined £10/19/6. Soon afterwards he and a few friends emigrated to Pennsylvania because of persecution. By 1721 a regular meeting place was found in Acresfield approximately where the Lloyds's TSB Bank stands in Hotel Street.

His brother Henry Ashworth joined him in developing the cotton trade but also was a land and property agent. Henry had two sons, John born in 1772 and Edmund born 1776, both of whom joined and continued the family cotton business, and in

1796 started to build the New Eagley Mills which opened for business in 1802. There was already an Eagley mill which was built in 1798 by John Wakefield. I assume the name New Eagley Mill was chosen because the mill drew its power in the form of a 17 feet waterwheel generating between 10 and 12 horsepower from Eagley Brook.

The mill was a three story building until it was extended in 1820 By adding more floors. Also nine cottages were built in the yard for some of the first 50 employees. Business was good and the mill was extended again to twice its size by 1828. The 17 feet waterwheel was replace by a 40 feet one generating 45 horse power.

As one looks at where the mills were built I feel it begs the question, why there? As the nearest main road is nearly a mile away and the approaches to the site would be a farm track from Blackburn Road. To reach the site from Tonge Moor Road there would need to be a road bridge across the brook and as far as I can make out there has only ever been a foot bridge.

This footbridge was probably been built by the Ashworths as part of the family lived at "The Oaks" on the east side of the brook. The only other approach to Ashworth Bottoms was from Birtenshaw and this track was also on the east side of the brook, and again there is only a foot bridge across the water. However on an old map of the area a ford is shown around the site of the present footbridge. Building a mill in what appears to be an inconvenient place would increase transport costs.

Another question did the Ashworths build or upgrade a country lane to become a cobbled Ashworths Lane? (Now Ashworth Lane). Obviously, to build the mill at Ashworth Bottoms would need a good road to carry all the heavy building materials and also machinery for the factory. I suppose if you look at the land it is reasonably flat with a brook running alongside for water power and most importantly did the land belong to the Ashworths in the first place.

There were many local footpaths and footbridges which cut down the amount of walking time it took workers to get too and from the mills, which I believe although I have no proof which were built or maintained by the Ashworths. From Birtenshaw there is a farm track leading towards New Eagley finishing at a footbridge over Eagley Brook which leads directly to the mill yard. From Tonge Moor Road, another farm track which passed The Oaks to a second foot bridge taking people again, straight into the yard. For people living in the lower part of Astley Bridge, a farm track left Blackburn Road to Old Nells farm meeting a track known as Old Wash which went north passed New House farm meeting a five barred gate about 100 yards from Lower house. Old Wash continued to Ashworth Lane, but just below Lower House a foot path from Rainshaw Street running between allotments on one side and hen pens and more allotments on the other crosses Old Wash making its way through West Glen which I have already mentioned on page 62. The footpath through the two meadows ends at Yew Tree Lane which takes you to Bank Top.

The whole operation was a great success and the brothers were hungry for more. An opportunity came for expansion when Philip Novelli was struggling financially at Egerton Mill. The brothers took over the mill. The mill was only about 3 miles from New Eagley being quite convenient for the brothers to manage, as there were a couple of ways to get from one mill to the other; one was Ashworth Lane – Blackburn Road and the other Birtenshaw – Darwen Road. In no time at all the brothers started to extend their new purchase. More power was needed for the increase in capacity so a new 62 feet waterwheel was installed generating over 110 horse power. The wheel was one of the largest in the country and not only generated a lot of power but also a lot of interest from visitors.

In 1830 Henry Ashworth like many other mill owners reduced wage rates when introducing larger machines. This caused resentments and strikes. One night a gang dressed in women's clothes attacked the village school breaking all the windows, then moved to attack the mill manager, however he escaped by climbing up a chimney.

In 1840 there was both concern and outrage in the Bolton newspapers and Parliament about Henry Ashworths treatment of his workers, because of his blunt and stubborn stand on, trade unions, rules on working, hours and free trade.

Rhodes Boyson in his book "The Ashworth Cotton Enterprise". Acknowges that piece work rates were 10% lower than the rest of Bolton. Wages were on average 33/- per week whilst the rest of the town paid between 25/- and 43/- in the 1830/40s. Whilst on the face of it the differences were small but this was an understatement as Henry fined his workers more than other Bolton employers.

Taking all the negatives into account i.e. wages and fines, the Ashworths wanted a better standard of living for their workers especially in education, and more people on average working for the Ashworths could read and write than any other parts of the town.

In the1830/50s the Ashworths built a number of cottages on Tops farm land, this gave the village its name as the mills were at the bottom of hill or bank below Tops farm hence the name

BANK TOP

HUGH LUPOS STREET

Around half the workers and their families lived in the cottages. A school was built in 1833 it was named "Sharples Ashworth British School". The school also housed the library. Eventually the building was converted into a private house (251Ashworth Lane) when the old Bank Top school was built. The school and library were originally sited in the mill building.

By 1871 Bank Top had 71 cottages of various sizes, 2 shops and a cricket field. In 1923 the Bank Top Tennis Clubhouse was built by the Ashworths and extended in 1935. It was quite a successful club in the Bolton area with three clay courts. In 1964/5 some male members got interested in playing Hockey and formed a team. Initially they played friendly games on the parks, and then they managed to get a base at Bolton Cricket Club. Times were changing; tennis was loosing its popularity with players numbers dwindling finally the club folded. The club house began to deteriorate, Mother Nature started to take over the courts and they soon became overgrown with vegetation. The whole complex soon became an eyesore in the village. Then in the mid 1990s John Feeney who had a brewery in Back Lane took over the pavilion and established Bank Top Brewery in 2003. Eventually the tennis courts were cleared and lawns and flower bed were laid, and the whole area is an asset to the village.

In their day these cottages were quite up market having piped water, gas, and each house had a yard with an outside lavatory. In those days many houses had to share the lavatory with other families, so having your own loo was a bonus. The average cost of building the cottages was between £80 and £140 and rents ranged from 1/6 to 4/3 per week which included rates, water, and gas. The higher paid employees like the spinners would get the bigger houses. There were also larger houses for mill managers the rents for these was 5/- per week. All the houses were regularly painted outside and decorated inside at the Ashworths expense.

According to a William Dodd who was a great critic of the factory system said that these houses were good substantial stone buildings, roomy, well drained, well lighted, with both a front and back door.

Although the workers earned less than other parts of Bolton they were prosperous even in the depression of the 1840s. People remarked on the material comforts of the Ashworth employees, not only that, there were apparently, high standards of health, sanitation and literacy.

However the benefits came with conditions. The Ashworths exercised strict supervision of their employees, drinking and keeping improper company could mean the sack, also the homes of the employees were inspected regularly or cleanliness, even down to furniture and bedding. The Ashworths also believed that workers living in a well kept house were probably more honest, reliable and trustworthy.

Bolton's housing in the 1830s was appalling, both the death rate and infant mortality rate were high. It was considered an exceptional privilege to rent an Ashworth cottage, and there were at least 20 applications when a cottage became vacant.

New Eagley mills had gardens and a hot house for vines and peaches. There was an orchard, summerhouse with a thatched Roof, a pond, and fountain. The Ashworths also planted shrubs in the cottages which had a garden.

In the mill was a library with over 1,500 books, and as I have already said the Ashworths were keen on education and would pay for employee's children to be educated.

A Lord Ashley who visited the mills was impressed with their position in a lovely valley with good fresh air, which was in great contrast to the filth and squalor of Bolton.

In 1880 the spinning mill closed and later reopened as a weaving mill with over a thousand looms, the number being increased to over 1,200 some time later.

LOOMS IN A WEAVING SHED I DO NOT KNOW THE LOCATION

During the last war the mill was close for the duration. The government decreed that over a third of all manufacturing had to close because of lack of labour and demand. It reopened after the war until 1949 when it closed for good.

The mill was demolished to be replaced with a lovely stone house and riding paddock and stables.

As more mills were built the labour market became more difficult for employers and eventually wage rates become somewhat standard throughout the industry.

Henry Ashworth was a tower of strength in the Anti Corn Laws League in 1839. The Corn Law was introduced in 1804 when the great landowners many of whom were members of Parliament wanted to protect their profits from being eroded by cheaper imports. This is what happened as the price of corn dropped from 126/6 a quarter in 1812 to 65/7 in 1815. The landowners were not happy and started to put pressure on the government. Parliament passed a new law permitting the import of foreign wheat free of duty when the price of wheat in this country reached 80/- a quarter.

The country was in uproar, and when the law was passed Parliament had to be defended by armed soldiers against a very angry crowd. Needless to say the landowners were rubbing their hands with glee with the new Corn Laws, but manufacturers were not happy as there could be demands for wage increases to offset the price of bread. This problem raised its head in 1816 when the harvest failed causing bread prices to rise rapidly. This caused strikes and riots all over the country, which led to the Anti Corn Law League being formed.

The League was made up mainly from middle class people such as manufactures, merchants and bankers, but even with people of this calibre and clout the laws were not repealed until 1846 by Sir Robert Peel.

During Henry's time as a member of the league he visited with other members the ruins of Tantallon Castle, when he came out with quite a prophetic statement. "How long will it be before our great warehouses and factories in Lancashire are a complete ruin as this castle" He admits that he has thought about this scores of times, thinking of it with sadness.

If ever they come to ruin they will never be as picturesque as Tantallon Castle.

Henry, being a Quaker did not stop him from taking part in one of his favourite pastimes, and that was game shooting. One of his great pleasures was to go onto the moors and bag some grouse.

Edmund and his brother Thomas were very keen, enthusiastic fishermen and in 1852 they bought the Galway Fisheries at a knock down price of £5000. The fisheries were in somewhat a sorry state, catches had been low and poachers did not help matters. The brothers brought their management and enterprising skills to the fisheries and set about turning round the fortunes of the company. With the help of Robert Ramsbottom from Clithero they stated to experiment with what we now call salmon farming, something that may have been tried before but without success. However between them they soon mastered the art of salmon rearing and in their first year they stripped eggs from female salmon which were then fertilised, and Professor N P Wilkins tells us that probably a fair representation of the operation was that out of the 24,000 eggs 20,000 hatched, salmon farming was born, Their success was noted by others and the science of aquaculture spread around the world.

The two brothers wrote a number of books on the subject
"A Treatise of the prorogation of salmon and other fish"
"Report upon the fisheries of Spain and Portugal"
Both of these were co- written by Edmund and Thomas
"The salmon fisheries of England 1868, written by Thomas.
The fishery was disposed of in 1922.

On the 30th June 1854, the following announcement was made in the "London Times"

"THE Partnership heretofore subsisting between the undersigned, Henry Ashworth and Edmund Ashworth, in the business of Cotton Spinners and Manufacturers, carried on at the New Eagley Mills, and also at the Egerton Mill, in the county of Lancaster, under the firm of H. and B. Ashworth, expired this day, by effluxion of time. The business at the Egerton Mill will in future be carried on by the said Edmund Ashworth, under the firm of Edmund Ashworth and Sons; and that at the New Eagley Mills will in future be carried on by the said Henry Ashworth, under the firm of Henry Ashworth and Sons, by which latter firm all debts due or owing to or by the late firm of H. and E. Ashworth will be received and paid."—Dated this 30th June, 1854.
Henry Ashworth.
Edmund Ashworth.

By 1867 there were possibly 700 people employed at New Eagley (During my research I found differing numbers of employees from 281 to nearly 1000)

Bank Top is a designated Conservation Area, with the original village having four streets running off Ashworth lane, namely Hugh Lupos, and Oulton on the side south and Eleanor, and Fitzburg, on the north. The school which opened in 1856 had the grand title of "The New British School at Bank Top" is now a private house and was replaced with the Sharples School County Primary which opened in 1969.
The 1856 school when operating, was also used as a community centre at weekends and in the evening. It had its own Scout and Guides section. During the winter months there was a dance every Saturday evening with local small bands playing for the enjoyment of the dancers. Many of the bands had new musicians

who were making a start in the music business probably with an eye to greater things such as, playing in the bands of the established dance halls like the Palais, Empress or the Aspin. Also there were greater goals for the outstanding musician of playing in the top bands of the country like Ted Heath, Geraldo and many more. Alyn Ainsworth the son of a plumber lived at the bottom of Blackburn Road played in Oscar Rabin's band and became the conductor/arranger of the BBC Northern Dance Orchestra started his career with a guitar in bands playing at church and club dances and the like.

At the side of the old school was Kay's farm whose land stretched to Ashworth Bottoms.

There were no beer houses or inns within a mile of the village in accordance with Ashworths Quaker tradition.

Eleanor Street a row of eight cottages faces what was the site of the tennis club. They were originally built as back to back dwellings. In 1900 they were converted to through houses. At the rear is Fitzburg Street which when built had six cottages. The tenants of these cottages were re-housed and the buildings were knocked through to make social club around 1900. Unfortunately through lack of use the building became derelict and neglected. In 1910 the Congregationalists came to Bank Top forming a church which met in the 1856 school. By 1926 the social club building had been refurbished and the Congregational church moved from the school into the building and took over the renovated premises. In 1972 the Congregationalist and the Presbyterian denominations joined together to become the United Reform Church, with 68,000 members, 1,500 congregations and nearly 700 ministers, both paid and unpaid.

Bank Top U.R.C is a well supported and thriving fellowship. Just outside of the church building stood two stout stone gatepost pillars, one on each side of the carriageway in Ashworth Lane, and whilst the road on the west side of the lane

202

to the Ashworths. Every year on 12th May a chain was hung from one post to the other, and any vehicle wanting to cross to the Ashworth owned part of the lane had to get permission to have the chain removed. Around the 1950s the rest of the lane was adopted and the gate posts were removed.

Henry Ashworth, born in 1728. Died 15th June 1789, and is buried in Bolton Parish Church. He was educated at the Quaker School in Ackworth, West Yorkshire, near Pontefract. When he was about 17 years old, his life as a Quaker life would not be too pleasant as many of the dissenters were made very uncomfortable in life. Meeting houses were attacked and burned by mobs of angry people who were for "Church and King". They went around the country terrorising the Radicals.

In 1662 a new Prayer Book was published by the Church of England, and the same year the "Act of Conformity" came into force. All clergymen were expected to conform to the doctrine of the new Prayer Book. However, not all clergy could accept the new diktat and the dissidents were thrown out of their livings. In fact 13 Vicars in the Bolton area could not, and would not accept the doctrines of the new prayer book and found themselves out of work, including the Vicar of Bolton Rev. Richard Goodwin, who had been in charge at the Parish Church from 1857. At this time, non- conformism was born and Bolton became one of the first and leaders in the new church movements, so much so, Bolton became known as the Geneva of the North, as a number of the newly formed denominations like Baptists, Quakers and Presbyterians who shared some, if not all of John Calvin's beliefs. Meetings outside the established church were more than frowned upon, but this did not stop people meeting and forming new groups. A new Act was passed called the Five Mile Act. Meaning if a meeting was held, there should be limited numbers and the preacher should not live within five miles of the meeting place. Obviously this was to deter preachers travelling what in the 1600s was a great distance. The non-conformists were not put off by the new regulation and would meet secretly in out of the way places to worship.

Eventually religious restrictions were rescinded when the Toleration Act came into force in 1689 and people could build their own churches and chapels and also worship at will. This gave rise to the building of Bank Street Chapel in 1696, although 1672 is generally accepted as the foundation year of the chapel with people prior to this date meeting in various places one of which was the home of John Okey who left Bolton Parish Church in sympathy with the Rev Richard Goodwin. His home was at the corner of Mealhouse Lane and Deansgate, where the Midland Bank stood. In 1695 Robert Seddon presented the land on which Bank Street chapel was built. Eventually the Presbyterians moved to their new chapel on Windybank (Bank Street) in 1696. By 1700 it had the biggest non-conformist congregation in Lancashire of over 1000 souls. Around 1750 there was a departing of the ways when people could not agree with some of the doctrine. A new church was built at Dukes Alley which became Congregational, leaving Bank Street Chapel to Unitarian Theology.

WALMSLEY UNITARIAN CHAPEL HISTORY.

Walmsley Chapel became a prime target for persecution even when the Toleration Act was passed. There was great antagonism from the Anglicans and some time later from the Congregational's. The Walmsley Chapel congregation was formed before 1672 as Presbyterians, and before the chapel was built would meet in secret at night in a wild and lonely spot call Yearnsdale Holmes. There were lookouts on duty to make sure that the authorities were not around.

The book "The story of Walmsley Chapel" tells us that a plot of land some 20 x 18 yards was bought for a new chapel from Christopher Horrocks for £7 and was subject to an annual ground rent of one penny payable on 25th December. The chapel itself measured 14 x 12 yards, for a number of years the floor wasn't flagged and there were no pews just forms with wooden backs. However the Horrocks family stipulated that no one could be interred either in the chapel or its grounds without their permission. In 1748, another 2 acres of land was bought from the Horrocks family for a £100 which included a house for the minister and land for a graveyard. On completion of this additional purchase, the prohibition of people being buried in the chapel, or its grounds were rescinded and payment of ground rent was relinquished. In 1745 the Presbyterians got wind of an attack to be carried out to destroy the chapel. Members of the chapel armed themselves with muskets and things which they could use to ward off an attack. They bored holes in the doors, and also took out small panes of glass so they could defend the building with their muskets. The mob, with people from Bolton and "Tum Fowt" arrived but decided against trying to attack the chapel with it being so well defended by farmers and their sons. The Congregationalists had their eye on the chapel, and on one occasion during a funeral at the chapel, the minister was conducting the service at the graveside when three Congregational clergy stayed in the chapel hoping to get the keys, however the chapel keeper very wisely carried the keys in his pocket. When he returned to the chapel after the funeral to lock up, he found the three ministers who refused to leave, so he threatened to lock them in all night whereupon they left. As time went by like Bank Street chapel the Walmsley chapel became Unitarian. The longest serving minister was Rev. William Probart who was the minister from 1821- 1871 and over this time the locals referred to the chapel as "Probert's Chapel"

PROBERT'S CHAPEL

John Ashworth was born in 1696 and was instrumental in starting the great cotton empire of the Ashworth family. In his early days he bought the raw cotton from Liverpool and sold or loaned the cotton to the local cottage cotton spinners, buying the spun cotton from them, and using the same principles he passed the cotton to the cottage weavers again paying them for the finished cloth.

His brother Henry Ashworth joined him in developing the cotton trade but also was a land and property agent. Henry had two sons, John born in 1772 and Edmund born 1776, both of whom joined and continued the family cotton business, and in 1796 started to build the New Eagley Mills which opened for

business in 1802. There was already an Eagley mill which was
built in 1798 by John Wakefield. I assume the name New
Eagley Mill was chosen because the mill drew its power in the
from of a 17 feet waterwheel generating between 10 and 12
horsepower from Eagley Brook.

The mill was a three story building until it was extended in 1820
by adding more floors. Also nine cottages were built in the yard
for some of the first 50 employees. Business was good and the
mill was extended again to twice its size by 1828. The 17 feet
waterwheel was replace by a 40 feet one generating 45 horse
power.

As one looks at where the mills were built I feel it begs the
question, why there? As the nearest main road is nearly a mile
away and the approaches to the site would be a farm track from
Blackburn Road. To reach the site from Tonge Moor Road there
would need to be a road bridge across the brook and as far as I
can make out there has only ever been a foot bridge.

This footbridge was probably been built by the Ashworths as
part of the family lived at "The Oaks" on the east side of the
brook. The only other approach to Ashworth Bottoms was from
Birtenshaw and this track was also on the east side of the brook,
and again there is only a foot bridge across the water. However
on an old map of the area a ford is shown around the site of the
present footbridge. Building a mill in what appears to be an
inconvenient place would increase transport costs.

Another question did the Ashworths build or upgrade a country
lane to become a cobbled Ashworths Lane? (Now Ashworth
Lane). Obviously, to build the mill at Ashworth Bottoms would
need a good road to carry all the heavy building materials and
also machinery for the factory. I suppose if you look at the land
it is reasonably flat with a brook running alongside for water
power and most importantly did the land belong to the
Ashworths in the first place.

There were many local footpaths and footbridges which cut
down the amount of walking time it took workers to get too and

from the mills, which I believe although I have no proof which were built or maintained by the Ashworths. From Birtenshaw there is a farm track leading towards New Eagley finishing at a footbridge over Eagley Brook which leads directly to the mill yard. From Tonge Moor Road, another farm track which passed The Oaks to a second foot bridge taking people again, straight into the yard. For people living in the lower part of Astley Bridge, a farm track left Blackburn Road to Old Nells farm meeting a track known as Old Wash which went north passed New House farm meeting a five barred gate about 100 yards from Lower house. Old Wash continued to Ashworth Lane, but just below Lower House a foot path from Rainshaw Street running between allotments on one side and hen pens and more allotments on the other crosses Old Wash making its way through West Glen which I have already mentioned on page 62. The footpath through the two meadows ends at Yew Tree Lane which takes you to Bank Top.

The whole operation was a great success and the brothers were hungry for more. An opportunity came for expansion when Philip Novelli was struggling financially at Egerton Mill. The brothers took over the mill. The mill was only about 3 miles from New Eagley being quite convenient for the brothers to manage, as there were a couple of ways to get from one mill to the other; one was Ashworth Lane – Blackburn Road and the other Birtenshaw – Darwen Road. In no time at all the brothers started to extend their new purchase. More power was needed for the increase in capacity so a new 62 feet waterwheel was installed generating over 110 horse power. The wheel was one of the largest in the country and not only generated a lot of power but also a lot of interest from visitors.

In 1830 Henry Ashworth like many other mill owners reduced wage rates when introducing larger machines. This caused resentments and strikes. One night a gang dressed in women's clothes attacked the village school breaking all the windows, then moved to attack the mill manager, however he escaped by climbing up a chimney.

In 1840 there was both concern and outrage in the Bolton newspapers and Parliament about Henry Ashworths treatment of his workers, because of his blunt and stubborn stand on, trade unions, rules on working, hours and free trade.

Rhodes Boyson in his book "The Ashworth Cotton Enterprise". Acknowges that piece work rates were 10% lower than the rest of Bolton. Wages were on average 33/- per week whilst the rest of the town paid between 25/- and 43/- in the 1830/40s. Whilst on the face of it the differences were small but this was an understatement as Henry fined his workers more than other Bolton employers.

Taking all the negatives into account i.e. wages and fines, the Ashworths wanted a better standard of living for their workers especially in education, and more people on average working for the Ashworths could read and write than any other parts of the town.

In 1880 the spinning mill closed, and by 1884 had become a weaving shed with over a thousand looms. By 1900 more looms were installed. In the mid 1920s the number of looms had been reduced and by 1949 New Eagley Mills closed.

Bank Top is in a conservation area which means that there are many restrictions on what house owners can and cannot do with their property. Brick paving is not allowed. Alterations should use materials which match existing matter. UPVC windows and doors are not acceptable. In fact renewing anything at the exterior of the house can be a problem.

Leaving Bank Top church and continuing to Blackburn Road we pass a short row of houses and come to Cherry Tree Lane and on to the Whitegate private housing estate which was built sometime after the last war. The Bolton Evening News reported on 3rd April 1937 that Astley Bridge had a new tip. This was just east of West Glen, and the source of the glen's Barley brook is water which drains off the land between Sharples Hall and Ashworth Lane goes through a tunnel under the road just near Whitegate Drive and makes its way through a valley to West Glen. On each side of the valley used to be hen pens and allotments. Also, on the west side of the valley   *alongside the* smallholdings is the Florence Avenue allotments which stretch to Lower House. The enthusiastic holders are quite proud of their plots and produce. Last year (2012) they had an open day to raise funds for Bolton Hospice.

FLORENCE AVENUE ALLOTMENTS

In Florence Avenue lived the author Arthur Catherall, a well known author of books for the more mature child.

ARTHUR CATHERALL

Arthur Catherall was born 6th February 1906
Married Elizabeth Benson in 1936
They had one son and a daughter
Arthur worked in the mill before becoming a writer
He served in the RAF 1940-45 in Bengal and Burma, he was also well travelled man not only in the Far East but also Europe and Africa. He crossed Lapland from the border of Russia to the coast of Norway, and made many trawler voyages to the coast of Iceland's fishing grounds. He was a very active man liking all sorts of outdoor pursuits, such as climbing, sailing and camping. The background to his life and experiences gave him a wonderful canvas for writing exciting stories.
He wrote over 50 books many of which had more than one edition, with titles such as "Duel in the Hills" "Jackals of the Seas" "Vibrant Brass" and many more. A number of his books have become collector's items. I understand that he did most of his writing in his garden shed.

As we continue to Blackburn Road we pass Popular Avenue, Primula Street, and Primrose Street where a very well known builder, J Arrowsmith had his premises and yard. I remember he stored quite a lot of timber which I believe used to stand for up to two years to weather.

After the war he built quite a number of houses at the bottom of what was Rainshaw Street on land which contained a few garages and allotments.

On the corner of Ashworth Lane and Blackburn Road was a temperance bar, come sweet and tobacconist shop. It is now an Estate Agent. Proceeding down the road passing Rainshaw Street there are a couple of shops the one on the corner was Murrays fruit shop and next door was William Harold Bateson butchers shop.

WILLIAM HAROLD BATESON

Mayor of Bolton 1961/2
His wife Hilda was mayoress
Born Grant Street Astley Bridge in 1897
Died 26th July 1967
Master Butcher

Educated at St Paul's Astley Bridge.
Worked as a clerk in a solicitors office
Then in the cashiers office at Dobson and Barlows.
Served in the 12th Lancers in the 1st WW
Captain and second in Command in Astley Bridge Home Guard
Councillor for Astley Bridge 1945
President and Treasurer of Astley Bridge British Legion
Captain of Dunscar Golf Club representing both Bolton and Lancashire
Vice President Astley Bridge cricket Club
Founder President of Sweetloves Operatic and Dramatic society.

In the same row was Astley Bridge Police Station and yard. The station, I believe was staffed during day with three constables and a sergeant. The sergeant was quite a portly man and his bike had double cross bars. In those days, and I am talking about the 1930s the police knew virtually every family on their patch. I well remember that the station was manned with at least one person for most of the day. One exception to this was school opening and closing time when all the policemen were on duty at road crossings. At holiday times before the last war it was common practice to call into the police station and tell the police your address and how long you will be away, this was noted and the police would keep an eye on your property. Should the station be closed there was a police telephone pillar at the front of the station. The top was triangular, on one side was a little door, and on opening the door you were automatically through to the central emergency services, and through a speaker you would immediately be asked the reason for your enquiry.
Unlike today there seemed to be police pounding their beat most of the time. Should the traffic lights breakdown within minutes a policeman was on point duty directing the traffic, whereas today if the lights fail it is every man for himself. But thinking about the subject, technology has moved on greatly and traffic light breakdowns are a rare occurrence today.

The police moved to a new building on Crompton Way, and although the police have moved out of Astley Bridge the new police station is known as Astley Bridge.

The old police station was taken over by John and Alison Howarth who opened Howarth's funeral Service in 1991. The reason they give is a fair one. The Co-operative Funeral Service have around 51 % of all the funerals in the country, and although the local Funeral Directors have *Joe Bloggs over the* door the business belongs to the Co-op. The Howarth's want to give the public a family service that is truly independent of the big companies.

Just below the Police Station is East Cottage which in the 30s *was owned by* T.E. Horner a cattle dealer. The cottage has quite a large walled garden, and I remember as lads we would climb onto the wall with the help of a gas lamp post which stood on the corner of Murton Terrace to see this beautiful garden. Due to its high wall it was sort of a secret garden. The only other way to see it was from the upstairs of the tram or bus.

Crossing Holly Street we come to a parade of shops where in the 1930/40s one could buy most things. First a shoe shop which became a cooked meat shop, them Williams decorating supply *shop who also had* another similar shop in Corporation Street which was in the Market Hall with two entrances one in the hall and the other in the street. Holden's the bakers came next followed by a couple of private houses then Brindles hairdressers, Bramwell's corsetieres, Tatham's fish and chip which became a wireless shop then a launderette. ironmongers, sweet, chip, florist, milliners, chemist, TSB bank, haberdashery, cake, butchers and finally the Pineapple Inn.

In the middle of this row of shops was a wheelwright works namely, *Isherwoods and Faircloughs* which was the only single storey building in the row. This workshop was quite unique as the front was on Blackburn Road, whilst the back was in Holland Street; however the workshop also covered the back street, which meant there was no through road for dustmen or coal men. Some time after the last war the firm closed down and the premises were taken over by a builder who put a second storey on the building.

Lomax ironmongers then a sweet shop lovingly known as Bets' came next, then a private house belonging to Miss Mary Mayoh, Grundy's fish and chip shop, Lingard's ladies hairdressers, which became Concrete Products finishing up after the war as Wolfe's florists, another private house then came Miss Gertrude Winstanley's milliners. Demaines chemist and optician. Scholes plumbers, with TSB moving in just after the war. TSB has since left and now the business is a bookies.

Nearly all the shops which I have mentioned have gone and replaced by fast food outlets, a betting shops etc. Alongside what is now a betting shop is a little guinnel being a short cut through to Holland Street.

Just below the guinnel was a drapers, followed by a fruiterers which became a wireless shop then Young's the bakers, Howarth's Butchers were next door, in fact this has been a butchers shop for well over 110 years, although everyone thought its days were numbered a few years ago when there was a tremendous explosion which nearly destroyed the building. Next door was a private house which has now been taken over for an extension to the Pineapple Inn.

The building of Crompton Way meant that a number of properties on Blackburn road had to be demolished to make way for the new road but before this happened there used to be a narrow dog leg lane just below the Pineapple which allowed people to get to Ashworths mill in Holland Street and also Astley Bridge cricket ground.

Crompton way/Blackburn Road junction has had a number of improvements since the last war, and with each change meant buildings were demolished. With the building of Crompton Way in 1928 four houses on the east side of Holland Street were pulled down together with buildings on Blackburn Road. After the narrow lane next to the *Pineapple Inn, the following were* demolished, a stone mason, a fruiterer, the Packhorse Inn, a fish and chip shop, (prior to this was the Manchester and Salford bank now RBS), and a confectioners. There was also a smithy at the rear of these buildings which also came down.

Further improvements were made at this junction the completion of Moss Bank Way in 1938, with the loss of Williams Deacons bank which was on the corner of what was Cavendish street and Blackburn Road. The bank relocated on to the opposite side of the road. At a later date more improvements followed and sadly the bank had to move again as what was a relatively new building together with two houses next and the number 10 bus terminus were removed to widen the exit from Crompton Way, whilst on the other side of Blackburn Road the writing was on the wall for the Grapes Inn, the Conservative Club, the Co-op boot and shoe shop, a greengrocers, a sweet shop, and a dry cleaners which all bit the dust. The road widening scheme was completed leaving a small car park where the Conservative Club and other buildings stood.

I can recall back in the old days as we called them, night-watchmen sitting in their very small huts by a glowing brazier on a cold winters evening keeping their eyes on unfinished road works. Also the traffic census takers and like the night-watchmen they sat in little huts which were usually placed in a convenient spot near to road junctions, safely on the pavement counting the cars as they passed.

We are now making our way on the final part of our journey which will take us to Newnham Street where we come to the end of the tour.

On the completion of Crompton Way, three houses stood between the new road and Dove Street. The middle one was used as the local public offices which the villagers called the Town Hall that was until a brand new Public Office was built in what was then Heywood Street. The house was eventually bought by a well known Astley Bridge physician and surgeon

Robert Cranna. Just about where these houses were stood a valve house which was connected to the service reservoir which was on land on which Lidl Supermarket now stands, here again this land belonged to Lord Wilton as did quite a lot of land in the area. . When Crompton Way was being constructed great service pipes were discovered which ran from the old reservoir to where the valve house stood.

We then come to Dove Street which is, for all intents and purposes a back street with just four gable end properties. How it got the name Dove Street is anyone's guess. In the 1930s a well known village grocer Mr Fred Dean had the first shop in another parade of shops. Later the shop was taken over by Mrs Halliday and eventually her son took charge, he bought Bennett's shoe shop next door, and then extended his shop. David halliday was very successful until the arrival of the Co-op which he could cope with, but ASDA came on the scene and things became more difficult. When he left he took a stall in the Ashburner Street market selling provisions and did extremely well.

As we make our way down the parade of shops, there was Miss Annie Gregory's hosiery, A temperance bar belonging to John Kay which became Shard's, Andersons general draper, Nuttall's draper and hosier, Gregory's sweet shop which I remember having quite up market fittings and fixtures, William Leach the hairdresser came next, unfortunately he got consumption and finished up in Wilkinson's Sanatorium for quite some time. Thomas Butterworth the dentist came next followed by four stone private cottages the first of which was taken over by Walsh's the corn merchants which was originally on the other side of the road facing Newnham Street. Howarth's watchmaker was the last in the stone buildings. Then came Mather's confectioners. John Carr butcher, Pendlebury's newsagents, and finally a chemist and optician Frank Hall. We cross Nell Street to a short row of four shops, these shops over the years seemed to have changed hands and trades more than others in Astley

Bridge. In 1892 the first property from Nell Street number 104 (now 504) was Jacksons newsagent, it then became the Bolton Co-op Reading Room later it became Hutchinson's bookmakers, 102 (502) was a milliners, then a confectioners, 100 (500) in 1892 was the Bank of Bolton, which has made three moves from here, first to number 593 Blackburn Road, taking over a dressmaker, then to 552 just across the road and finally down to the corner of Newnham Street. When the bank moved the shop became a dressmakers. Quite a coincidence that a dressmaker became a bank, and in turn a bank became a dressmakers, and also where the present Bank of Scotland is situated it is only about 30 or so yards from the original site even after three moves. Number 498 has also had more than a handful of changes in its time. As we cross what was Church Street now Birley Street which was named after Rev A Birley MA vicar of St Paul's 1859 to 1869. We come to what is now the Four Seasons café. Prior to the café there were three businesses on the site, the first was a sweet shop, the second a saddlers and the third was a cloggers. Then came a narrow back street followed by two private houses. Eventually Williams Glynn's as it was then, bought the houses and built the present bank on the land including the narrow back street. We are now at Newnham Street which used to be School Street.

ADDENDUM
PAGES NUMBERED 171 to 190
To replace
136 to 148
I am presuming that this is what Norman
intended to do. AR .

MOSS BANK WAY

Moss Bank Way is the newest main road in Astley Bridge. The building of this new road was completed in 1938, prior to this there was no actual through road to Heaton. Even getting to the top of Halliwell wasn't easy for vehicles, be they horse and carts or motor. *To get there was anything but direct.* From Blackburn Road you turned into Cavendish Street to Sharples Park, past Thornleigh, then left turn into Oldhams lane down to Moss Lea where there was, and still is a cart track, turning right up the track to Harricroft farm where you do a dog leg turn past two very old cottages one of which had a hand imprint on one of the stones near the door. Turn left past the Coaching House onto Smithills Deane Road.

Should you be walking at the crossroads of Sharples Park and the top of Berkely Road *there was a foot path on the left taking* you towards what was Eden's Orphanage. The footpath then turned right which was called by the locals the "mile o' boards" which was a very long and high solid wooden fence. As you walked alongside the fence it seemed to go for miles. At the end was Moss Lea where you could take a footpath which led you to a jiggling bridge over the brook to Temple Road which in it turn brought you to the top of Halliwell.

To try not to cause too much confusion, before the 1900s Heywood Street went from Blackburn Road to the junction of Broad O'th Lane and Sharples Park, When Astley Bridge joined Bolton the name Heywood Street was changed to Cavendish Street and it wasn't until 1938 that there was a connecting road from Halliwell to the Broad O'th Lane/Sharples Park junction and then onto Blackburn Road when Cavendish Street by name only became a memory.

On Cavendish Street were the Public Offices dating from 1896 which replaced the old Astley Bridge Council Offices at 548 Blackburn Road. Later this address was better known as Doctor Cranna's surgery.

PUBLIC OFFICES OPENED 1896

The Farnworth journal dated Saturday 20th May 1876 reported that the health of the district during the past month had been satisfactory, one death from whooping cough, four from chest infections two from convulsions in children and one from kidney disease, the returns for March one from typhoid, one from small pox six from chest infections, and five from convulsions.

Behind the public offices was the Astley Bridge Maintenance Yard until 1948 when it eventually became EBM wholesale building supplies.

During the last war an Air Raid Wardens Post was built on the Blackburn Road side of the Public Offices. The post was usually occupied by volunteer Air Raid Wardens who patrolled the streets during air raids and in the hours of darkness, they made sure that everyone's blackouts were secure. Should a light be showing the standard "put that light out" was shouted to the offender. As a lad I remember going into the ARP post which seemed to be quite cosy. The wardens had a carpet square which had seen better days the floor. There was also a second hand settee and a table and chairs. The wardens were volunteers and spent some time in the Post when they weren't patrolling the streets. They were also responsible for directing civilians to the air raid shelters.

On the top of Heskeths mill was an air raid warning siren. When the siren gave an up an down sound that was a warning of a possible air raid attack, when the situation became safe from attack the all clear would sound, and that was a constant note from the siren. As you might expect the sirens were very loud.

From 1900 part the Public Offices housed the library; this was until the new Carnegie library was built next door, which opened on 29th September 1910. It was paid for by Mr Carnegie, as was Halliwell and Great Lever libraries which also opened on the same day. The Public Offices is now called Nationwide House, housing the offices of Nationwide Capital Finance Ltd, and her sister company. Franking Sense Ltd. They amongst other things supply Postal Franking Systems

ASTLEY BRIDGE LIBRARY

174

The foundation stone of Astley Bridge library was laid by Alderman Horridge on 29th September 1909.

Mr Archibald Sprake came to Bolton as Chief Librarian in 1904; on his arrival he was not at all happy with the organisation, but also on the choice of books.

He started to re-organise the library operation and Astley Bridge was to be the guinea pig for the exercise. He got plenty of brickbats with his plans, however attitudes changed as the success of the project came good, and as a result Bolton became a training ground for librarians. Sadly whilst the building is still standing the library closed on Thursday 5th April 2012.

In the review of 2011, we are told that the annual cost of the library was £67,956, there were 80,346 transactions, made up of 26,550 visitors, 11,542 enquiries, and 42,254 issues. The cost per transaction was 85p. The total book stock was 14,797.

I have been a member of Astley Bridge library since about 1935 and in that time I have seen a number of changes in the layout. The library was originally in three sections, the reading room, the adults department, and the children's department.

I went to St. Paul's School and I remember going straight to the library from school. In those days after 4 o'clock the children used a different entrance to the adults department and usually the desk was staffed with one of the more junior assistants, who carried the boxes of children's library book cards and tickets from the main desk to the children's desk ready for business "SILENCE PLEASE" notices were displayed in all sections of the building. It did not pay to make a noise as the assistants would give you a hard stern glare followed by a "shush" and "be quiet."

One memory I have is that of being intrigued by the large map of Astley Bridge which in those days hung on the wall opposite to where it is now in the entrance hall.(prior to the library closing) In its earlier position it was placed higher up on the wall which I feel was much better as the more populated parts of the village were nearer to eye level. For some reason the map was taken down and was out of sight for some time. I thought that the map had gone for good. Then the map returned and was as I have already said hung on the opposite wall, from then until the library closed if you want to look at what was the centre of the village 50 to 60 years ago you have to get down on your knees.

I use the map as a very good bible of the boundary of the Astley Bridge village, as it was drawn up in 1911when Mr. Archibald Sparke was the Chief Librarian and as I have already said his attention to detail was second to none.

The reading room which became part of the main body of the library was a "no go" area for children if unaccompanied. However on the few occasions I managed to peep into the room I was fascinated with the slanting desks which held mainly broadsheet newspapers. The newspapers were fastened to the desks by highly polished brass rod.

Also available were various magazines in special folders. These were usually found on the many tables in the reading room. One thing that I do remember was that during the day, especially in winter, were a number of men who were out of work, or retired not only enjoyed reading the newspapers but also meeting up

176

with their friends for a quiet chat in a nice warm room. There was also a ladies reading room which was much smaller than the main reading room, however this room became the day room for the library assistants.

Before the days of computers people were allowed to take up too four books out at a time. When an adult joined the library they were issued with four buff coloured open pocket type tickets. The people then chose their books and went to the counter where the librarian would date stamp a special page at the front of the book, then take out a card from a pocket which was on the inside cover of the book. The card contained details of the book, such as the title, author, and shelf number. The card was then inserted into the pocket of the library ticket and filed away in a long narrow box. People were allowed to keep the book for two weeks after which, should the book not be returned in the allotted time a fine was imposed, and the longer a person held the book the bigger the fine.

Astley Bridge library is a fine and elegant building and when built must have been quite modern for the time with very large plate glass windows built into the dividing walls, and also a wonderful roof with beautiful leaded light windows covering just under a third of the ceiling all of which helped to give maximum light. Inside the building are two wonderful leaded light and stained glass windows depicting coats of arms.

The library was used for many community projects. The Astley Bridge Area Forum was held regularly here where the residents could meet with their three council representatives and hear first hand at what was going on regarding the district, and also people could question and also bring to the councilors notice problems arising in Astley Bridge.

Local schools used the library for many projects.

With the closing of the library, the Forum Meetings are held in the Baptist Church in Eden Street, as is the Reminiscence Group meetings who use to meet on the 1st Tuesday afternoon in the month. The meetings are now held on the 2nd Monday of the month. The group is made up of a cross section of ages, but mainly older, and discuss and reminisce about many subjects but most of all Astley Bridge history.

On the building of Moss Bank Way the pavement outside the library had to be taken back. Close to the building was an area which was fenced off because there was a drop of around six to eight feet allowing light into the cellar. This was filled in and became the new pavement, at the same time there were some handsome gate posts which were also taken down. I can recall the caretaker in my school days. He was Mr. Atherton, his son Brian was a classmate at St Paul's school.

The library building is part of Astley Bridges heritage

Sadly the library closed for good on10th April 2012, with some of its services being transferred to Oldhams Children Centre in Forfar Street. The centre has a number of uses for the community such as Yoga, Play Sessions, Clinics, Neighbourhood Collections, Health Visiting team, Café, Midwifery Etc.

Next to the library was a piece of derelict land facing Manley Terrace. I just wonder, should there have been another terrace facing the existing one, and if so what happened, did the builder go bankrupt. This land eventually became the home of Astley Bridge Conservative Club. The club had to move because of road widening at the Blackburn Road end of Moss Bank Way. Obviously there is plenty of political activity especially at election times, like the British Legion Club on Belmont Road it is a social club for the village.

178

ASTLEY BRIDGE PARK

Astley Bridge Park was opened on 27th April 1901 by Col. George Hesketh, and whilst not being a large park, it is well used. In the 1930s, the children's playground had swings, a helter skelter slide, rocking horse, swings, and a couple of other roundabouts. The play area has been upgraded all the old equipment has gone.

There were two well used tennis courts, both of which have gone, one became a basket ball court whilst the other was demolished and grassed over. Sometimes, when you went to the office which was in the bowling green pavilion to book and hire a court, there could be a waiting time of two hours to get on the court. There always seemed to be a park keeper on hand taking payment for both tennis and bowls. There was no extra charge for the hire of the bowls the cost was included in the price per hour. There was a large grassed play area and still is, suitable for football, cricket, rounders, and many other games. The bowling green was sacrosanct to the older men in 1930s and 40s. there did seem to be a clique amongst some of the bowling fraternity. If we, as teenage lads had to wait for an hour for a tennis court, we would spend some time on the bowling green. Some of the bowlers thought that we were pains in the neck, and looking back I can understand why.

The reason was, that we had no idea about the bias on the bowls, we could not read the green and more often than not would bowl quite short, which left our woods in the middle of the green much to the annoyance of some of the bowlers because we were spoiling their game. One or two of the older men would kindly come over and try to teach us how to bowl.

One thing that the crown green bowlers did that impressed people, and I believe that they are still doing today, and that is when a funeral passes they stop bowling and face the cortege as it passes should any of the bowlers be wearing a hat they will take it off, which shows a great mark of respect.

The park was a good well patronised outdoor community centre and was a great asset to the people both young and old. Sometimes the lads would sort themselves out into two teams put their coats down as goal posts and get on with a game of football. The girls would do a similar thing when playing rounders; they would use their coats as corner posts.

At the entrance to the park the flower beds were filled with a lovely display of colourful flowers. There were also some forms facing the flowers where usually you found the older people sitting and enjoying the scene. On many occasions these people would be licking an ice cream cornet or a slider (today we call them wafers.) which they had bought from the ice cream cart standing just outside the park gates.

At the entrance to the park were some wonderful displays of flowers in very attractive shaped flower beds. The Parks department had their own gardeners with greenhouses in Moss Bank Park. Roy Lancaster *served his time learning his* horticultural trade in Bolton. The park keeper's house was on the corner of Cavendish Street and Broad O'th Lane. One amazing thing about the park keepers was that if a child was a little mischievous by walking on the grass, which had a little notice "Keep off the Grass" the park keeper seemed to come out of the woodwork to tell the child off.

HOLY INFANTS AND ST. ANTHONYS

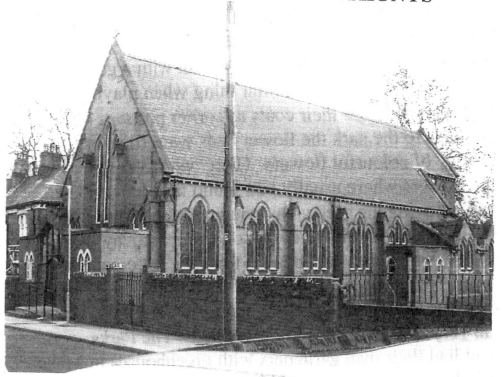

After the war, a piece of the park was taken to build a new Roman Catholic Holy Infants School which opened in1965, and was extended in 1972. This area was known as Spring Bank this was where a number of cottages used to stand many years before.

On Wednesday 9th August 1848 the Catholics celebrated the opening of a new church in Salford, St John the Evangelist. There were many bishops and priests and a congregation of about 1,600 in attendance.

Pope Pius 1X re-established the Catholic Diocese on 29th September 1850. On 25th July 1851 St. John the Evangelist church in Salford was made a Cathedral when the first bishop Doctor William Turner a Lancastrian from Whittingham was consecrated, he died whilst in office on 13th July 1872. The current Bishop is the Right Reverend Terence John Brain. He was appointed Bishop of Salford 2nd September 1997.

Before Holy Infants and St Anthony church was built, Astley Bridge and other areas in north Bolton were in the parish of St

Marie's in Palace Street. This was a large parish taking in not only Astley Bridge, but also Halliwell and Egerton.

St Marie's was bursting at the seams, and the church was greatly overcrowded, also in winter especially for the elderly it would be very difficult to make the journey. Trams did not start to operate until the 1880s, and only the more wealthy people would own a pony and trap

J A Hilton tells us in his book "Catholic Lancashire" that the Irish immigrant population between 1841 & 51 nearly doubled to over 191,000, and in1851 17% of Manchester's population were Irish. However by 1881 the figure was down to 7.5%, this wasn't because many of them had left but probably because of an influx of people coming from the rural and country areas to work in the booming city. This would also reflect on Bolton's population.

It was decided to build a chapel of ease in Astley Bridge, which opened 22nd August 1877. This was a big help to many Roman Catholic worshipers.

In 1874 a plot of land was bought for £47 which at one time was a brick yard, and a new school and chapel were built. The new mission of Holy Infants and St Anthony was born. The first priest was Fr Maximillion who lived at Park View. Times were bad for the parishioners who were few and very poor.

In its day the new chapel filled its roll, and in 1882 the day school started. In the schools early days the children could start work half time at ten years old. In November 1934 there was an epidemic of scarlet fever; In November 1936 the fog was so bad the school was closed. In 1940 heavy snow caused a poor attendance with only 94 pupils attending on the Monday, but this dropped to just 34 on the Tuesday, so the school closed for the rest of the week. The building was three stories high partly built on stilts which gave the playground a covered extension. The next floor was the school, and the third floor was the chapel. As more mills and other forms of industry came to the village there was an influx of people to work in the new industries. In 1894 Fr A M Vantonne came to the chapel and during his time the church was built and opened in 1902. A nice gesture in

recognition of his work made by the council was to name an Astley Bridge street after him. With the building of the church, it meant that the school could take up the worship area on the third floor.

However with Astley Bridge people, and housing increasing in number, there was a need for a new school. Not only was the old school too small, but the facilities were out dated and needed replacing. The new school was built after the war. The old building was taken down and the area is now used as a car park. When you look at the site where the old building stood in its latter days, you get the impression what a small area the building covered and also the feeling that there must have been plenty of overcrowding.

Although I lived in Astley Bridge for 27 Years in all that time I never saw the inside of the church. I finally had the privilege of going inside. I was attending a friend's funeral, and what a surprise I had. It is a beautiful village church with very striking and lovely stained glass windows, which not only let the light flood in but also light up the church with their brightness.

The rows of terraced houses in Mitre Street, and one side of Baxendale Street are still standing, but the terraced houses on Drummond Street, Major Street, Warwick Street, Baber Street, Maxwell Street, and the east side of Baxendale Street have all been demolished. As was the Belle Cinema which was destroyed by fire.

I remember that just before the war, the terrace of red brick houses in Maxwell Street were condemned, however due to the war the houses were saved, and I believe that they were taken off the condemned list. A landlord who owned most, if not all the houses sold all he owned for £50 each. A lot of the houses realised over a thousand pounds when resold.

On the land now stands 52 Bungalows (1, 2, &3 bedrooms) built in 1985 and houses people aged 60 and over. There is a community centre with lounge and garden. Some meals are available which are cooked on premises, there is a community alarm system, and regular social activities. The bungalows are rented and the organisation responsible is "Bolton at Home".

On the North West corner of what was T M Heskeths mills is now Hillview Court. This comprises of a number of apartment blocks and houses. Running between Hillview Court and the Asda supermarket is Hillview Road and on this road is a branch of the HSBC Bank.
There is also an area for the collection of bottles, tins, paper and cloths for recycling.

HESKETH'S LODGE AND HILLVIEW COURT

The building of Moss Bank Way caused a fair amount of disruption with the addition of two extra carriageways.
I have already mentioned Astley Bridge Cricket Club and the Thorns losing land. Also the end house in Manley Terrace and

Williams Deacons Bank on Blackburn Road were bought by compulsory purchase in order to facilitate road widening The bank relocated on the opposite side of Blackburn Road. Pavements were moved back in front of the park, library, and the public offices.

Eventually further improvements were needed to the busy crossroads of Blackburn Road and Crompton Way/ Moss Bank Way, and a number of buildings on the west of Blackburn Road had compulsory purchase orders on them. The Grapes Inn, Astley bridge Conservative Club which as said, relocated with a new building on derelict land facing Manley Terrace.

The Co-op boot and shoe shop which I used on many occaisions.

I, like most of the other children wore clogs both for school, and playing out with my friends. Clogs had either rubber, or iron soles and heels attached to the wooden base. Both the sole and the heel were fashioned like a horse shoe covering just the edge of the wooden sole.

You could get a number of designs; some clogs were lace ups whilst others had a clasp fastening. The former could be in the style of a boot or shoe, made with wooden sole and leather uppers and were fastened with a cord or leather lace. The latter was more of a slip on type of clog with a metal clasp fastening across the instep. All clogs had a piece of metal protecting the toe where the wooden sole met the leather uppers.

Clogs were very comfortable and quite warm. The thick wooden soles gave excellent insulation to the feet in cold and frosty weather. As a lad I wore the clasp rather than the lace up type. The reason being was that they were easier to put on. It was just a matter of sliding your foot into the clog and a flick of the clasp to fasten them rather than the long winded lacing up.

I and most of my friends preferred clogs with iron rather than rubber soles. There were a number of reasons for this. We could hear the clatter of our feet. We also enjoyed making sparks, by kicking the iron sole with a sliding action on the flagged pavement, also with iron soles we could slide on good smooth macadam. In winter they were ideal for sliding on ice and snow. They had one drawback in snow because as you walked over fresh snow, there was a build up of snow on the sole of the clogs which made you feel that you were walking on stilts. Sometimes the compacted snow would be up to six or more inches thick.

Although I said that this was a drawback, we used to see who could get the thickest pad of snow on our clogs before it finally came off. There were times when the pad of snow fell from one clog only, and we laughed as one of us would walk as though one leg was longer than the other.

With just the normal wear and tear our iron soles would last quite a long time before needing re- ironing. However, the sliding and making sparks meant that the irons wore out very quickly. I remember my parents telling me on more than one occasion to be more careful, as money did not grow on trees, and that I would not need my clogs repaired as often if I stopped sliding in them and making sparks.

When my clogs needed repairing, my mother gave me four pence to have them re-ironed, i.e. both soles and heels. Off to the "Stores" shoe shop I would go. The door of the shop creaked as you pushed it open. The shop was dim and dismal. There wasn't a great deal of light coming from the windows, because of a partition behind the window display. In the window, boots, shoes and clogs were displayed. On the partition were stuck posters advertising not only footwear, but also a range of Pelaw Polishes. The posters kept a lot of the natural day light from coming into the shop. To augment the little daylight available, there were a couple of electric lights with dusty green glass shades, one at the front and the other at rear end of the shop. The power of these lamps could be no more than 100 watts each, unfortunately the lamps were covered in fly dirt which did not help in illumination.

The smell as you walked in was another memorable thing. It

186

was a mixture of new leather, wood, and polish. The floor was well worn, with the knots in the floor boards protruding quite a lot due to the wear and tear the floor had taken over the years. The main culprit for this was probably clogs.

The counter was a long and dark coloured with plenty of scratches, and chips in its surface. At each end of the counter stood a glass case containing boot polishes, laces, and other footwear brick-a-brack.

I asked the assistant if I could have a new set of clog irons fitted whilst I waited. "Yes that will be four pence please," he replied. I paid for the repair; he put the money in a cash drawer, then wrote out a paper check for four pence. I put it safely away. The book the assistant used was full of perforated checks. It was housed in a metal tray like contraption. When I got home, the check would be put with others in a jam jar in the cupboard. They stayed there until someone found the time to stick them on the official Co-op gummed sheet. The sheet enabled my mother to get her Co-op dividend (divi) at the end of the Financial Quarter. Finally, the shoe shop assistant gave me a metal token which, when presented to the cobbler authorised him to repair my clogs. The assistant then told me to go upstairs and to wait my turn to see the cobbler.

The stairs were at the rear of the shop. They were very rickety, and the hand rail seemed to be a little dodgy, however I still held the tightly as I ascended the well worn and poorly lit steps. There was no way anyone could surprise the cobblers because each step creaked as it was stepped on.

The stairs led to the workshop where one or sometimes two cobblers wearing leather aprons sat at a large workbench which always seemed to be cluttered, even so, the cobblers could lay their hands on anything without any trouble. Again, the workshop like the shop itself was very poorly lit. The lights hanging low over the bench cast long shadows around the room. "Sit down," said one of the cobblers. There was a row of bentwood chairs facing the cobblers bench. It was like going to the barbers as there may be other people waiting to have their clogs repaired. As each person got their newly soled clogs everyone moved up to the next seat. When you got on the end chair one of the cobblers would call "Reight lad, let mi have thi token and thi clugs," I gave him the token, and slipped off my clogs. Handing them to him, he put one on his last and proceeded to prise the old irons off the wooden soles with a pair of pincers. (There were times when the irons were so badly worn they would already be in pieces.) He then plugged the holes where the nails had been with little wooden pegs which were similar to a match stalks.

Taking a new iron he lined it up with the sole, put in a nail or maybe two to keep it steady, then with a hammer would shape the iron to the wooden sole, just like a blacksmith shoeing a horse. This done he finished nailing the iron to the wooden sole. He repeated the procedure with the heel, and the other clog. Incidentally whilst he was fitting the irons he kept the nails in his mouth taking the nails as he required them. The final job was to rub the outside of the sole with a piece of emery paper, and "the job was a good un."

On went my clogs which felt a lot different with the new irons. There was just one more thing to do to check that the newly soled and heeled clogs were right.

This could only be done outside, and it was to give the pavement a sliding kick to make sure that the new irons would give off sparks. This test done satisfactorily, I went happily on my way.

Next door to the Co-op was Sally Wilkinson's green grocers, then a sweet shop, dry cleaners, private boot and shoe shop, together with a grocers shop. All these properties had be demolished to make way for further road improvements. These shops were very busy in their day. For many years the grocery shop was run by the Wilkinson family together with another shop at the corner of Waterloo Street and Blackburn Road.

Sally one of the daughters then took over the green grocers a few years before the road improvements.

There is now a small car park where some of these buildings stood, many people do not realise that it is there as there is no direct access from Moss Bank Way. To use the car park you have to turn off Moss Bank Way into Drummond Street or Manley Terrace, then right into Warwick Street towards Belmont Road then right again down a back street just after the electricity sub station.

BELMONT ROAD

We continue our journey up the west side of Belmont Road. Due to the crossroad alteration the first house on this side was demolished. The old Co-op branch number 12 stood at the corner of Warwick Street, next door was the Co-op butchers department. It was here where my mother did most of her shopping. I remember my dad bringing his wage packet home every Friday, and then started the great divide. First my dad got his spending money, then the rent money, the newspaper money, the milk money, finally the club chaps money (insurance man). The rest my mother kept for housekeeping. After we had had our tea I would go with my mother to the stores (Co-op) to do the weekly shopping. The shop was always busy on Thursday and Friday evenings and sometimes we were there for nearly and hour.

However not all was lost as whilst customers were waiting they shared the local gossip, such as have you heard about so and so's daughter? She having a baby but we don't know who the father is! or another topic was, so and so is marrying a catholic or such a body is marrying a protestant, or someone has run away with another mans wife. In those days these were the highlights of gossip.

I did like to go with my mother, not for the gossip as for most of the time it was above my head. But I was fascinated to see the men behind the counter cutting cheese, and weighing other provisions and also the way the assistants wrapped things up. Slicing Bacon and cooked meats on the slicing machine was another thing I liked to watch, as at times, the man if slicing boiled ham would give you a little piece then ruffle your hair. Another thing which amazed me was the way in which they would parcel groceries in brown paper if the customer had not brought a bag. For some reason my mother always went to Howarth's butchers on Blackburn Road for the meat.

Continuing up Belmont Road after the Co-op shops were a number of stone cottages, some of which were taken down when the *Drummond Street community bungalows* were built. The row of bungalows facing Belmont Road had a garden with lawn and bushes, unfortunately the gardens were a dumping ground for cans and bottles, and also fast food waste. Due to this nuisance a high "see through" metal fence was built with a gateway in the middle. For some time there was no gate on the opening and the residents still got a lot of rubbish in the front of their houses.

Eventually very decorative wrought iron gate was made; the theme of this gate is a sort of reminder and a potted history of old time recreation in the village. Certain motives are worked into the gates construction. For instance---

The initials of D. S. R. A. denote Drummond Street Residents Association.

The motto on the gate is "Gang Warily" which is the motto of the Drummond Clan. The motto means "Go Carefully"

Film and Cans remind us of the Belle Cinema.

Birds depict the ducks and swans on Hesketh's and Ashworth's Lodges

Dancers represent frequent dances at St Paul's Parochial Hall, and also at Bank Top School each Saturday evening during the winter months.

Although this gate is reasonably new it is already part of the heritage of Astley Bridge

There was an official opening of the new gate by the Mayor Mr John Walsh 11th December 2002. *quite a number of people* attended to witness the occasion, unfortunately the Bolton Evening News should have been there to record the event but sadly did not make it.

BIRLEY STREET
CONSERVATION AREA

B·O·L·T·O·N
M·E·T·R·O

Environment Department

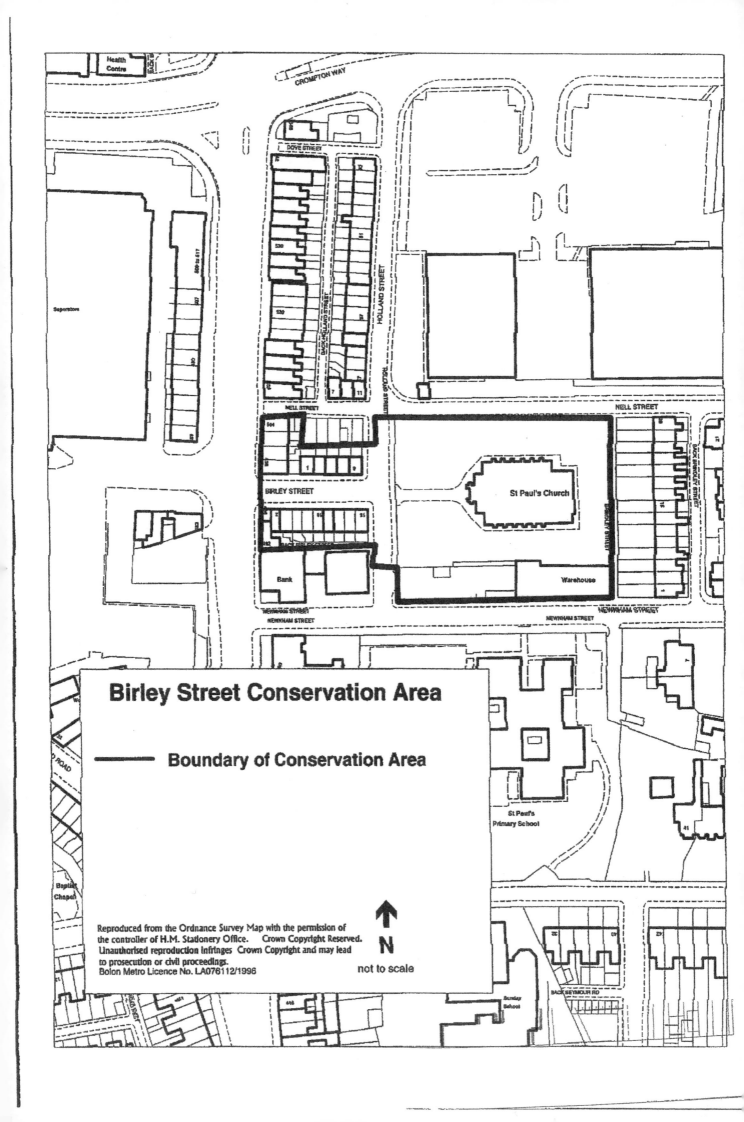

Birley Street Conservation Area

——— **Boundary of Conservation Area**

N

not to scale

CROMPTON WAY

DOVE STREET

HOLLAND STREET

BACK HOLLAND STREET

HOLLAND STREET

NELL STREET

NELL STREET

BIRLEY STREET

BACK BIRLEY STREET

BIRLEY STREET

St Paul's Church

Warehouse

Bank

NEWNHAM STREET

NEWNHAM STREET

NEWNHAM STREET

Superstore

Health Centre

BACK BIRLEY STREET

St Paul's
Primary School

Baptist
Chapel

ROAD

BACK SEYMOUR RD

Sunday
School

SECTION ONE

Character Assessment

Introduction

The Birley Street Conservation Area is situated in the Astley Bridge District, 1.5 miles north of Bolton Town Centre, and is located off the main Blackburn Road (A666). It consists of two groups of commercial buildings fronting Blackburn Road, two terraces of houses on Birley Street, St. Paul's Church the former St Pauls Infant School and the southern end of Holland Street. The buildings date from the mid 19th Century.

History

Astley Bridge was originally an agricultural settlement completely separated from Bolton by open countryside. It grew up where the main road from Bolton to Blackburn crosses the Astley Brook, a tributary of the River Tonge. The name Astley is possibly derived from "ast" meaning east or ash and "lay" an Old English work for an "open place in a wooded area" It could therefore mean "the clearing in the east" or "the clearing among the ash trees".

Textile production began in Astley Bridge in the 17th Century as a domestic industry, largely as a result of the enterprise of John Ashworth. The Ashworth family came from London to Bolton in 1665. John Ashworth bought cotton in Liverpool and Manchester, distributed it to local cottage spinners and weavers and marketed the finished cloth. This provided a welcome income for local people in an area which was of poor agricultural quality. The business flourished and the Ashworths and neighbouring gentry became manufacturers.

Henry Ashworth (1728 - 1790) was a major figure in the development of the local cotton industry and after his death his two sons John and Edmund carried on the family business. In 1803 the Ashworths built their first major mill, New Eagley on the banks of the Eagley Brook. In 1892 Henry and Edmund purchased Egerton mill, extended it and installed a 62ft water wheel. Between 1862 and 1864 John Ashworth founded his own cotton spinning firm and in 1865 opened New Mill on Holland Street. By this time the mills were powered by steam and no longer needed to be located in the river valleys. As a result Astley Bridge developed rapidly into an industrial and residential settlement during the second half of the 19th Century.

The road to Blackburn was originally a meandering track, unfit for traffic in winter, until it was taken over and improved by the Bolton and Blackburn Turnpike Trust, at the end of the 18th Century. The toll gate was situated where Bar Lane meets Blackburn Road.

St. Pauls Church was built at the heart of Astley Bridge in 1848 at a cost of £4,000, to accommodate 745 people. It was extended in 1868 to accommodate 1,168 people. The site of the church and burial ground were a gift from the Earl of Wilton. Early benefactors of St. Pauls Church and Schools were the Ashworth Family and other prominent local people including the Greenhalgh brothers of Thornydyke, Thomas Thwaites of Watermillock, Sir John and Lady Holden and Colonel George Hesketh.

Birley Street, leading to the church was originally called Church Street, but as there was already a road of that name in Bolton, it was renamed after the Reverend A Birley, Vicar of St. Pauls between 1858 and 1869.

The stone houses on Birley Street and Blackburn Road were built shortly after the church, probably for mill workers.

In the early 19th Century the parish had a day school called the Penny School and there was a Sunday School by 1840. This accommodation was soon inadequate and a school teacher's house had been built by 1858. By 1871 there was an infants school and a girls school was built in 1881. A Parochial Church Hall was completed in 1915.

Astley Bridge was incorporated into Bolton by the Extension Act of 1898 but retained much of its independence and did not lose its District Committee of an alderman and three councillors until 1950.

Townscape

The Conservation Area consists of two distinct forms of development; the tightly built terraced houses on Blackburn Road and Birley Street and St. Pauls Church located in the centre of a burial ground. This landscaped area is an important open green space in a densely developed area of terraced housing.

Blackburn Road is wide and open and carries a heavy amount of vehicular traffic, being a major route in and out of the Town Centre. It is also well used by pedestrians because it contains a wide variety of shops and services.

Birley Street and Holland Street are more narrow and much quieter, being residential roads. In spite of alterations to the buildings, the St. Pauls Conservation Area has retained much of the character of a mid 19th Century residential district and industrial community.

Enclosures

There are clear views along Blackburn Road towards the Town Centre to the south and to Astley Bridge in the north. There is a view westwards from Birley Street across a car park, of the housing area beyond Blackburn Road. The view eastwards along Birley Street is terminated by St. Pauls Church with its prominent tower and spire. The church forms the focal point of the area and the tower and spire are a local landmark.

The terraced properties front directly onto the footpath. St. Pauls Church is bounded along Holland Street and Nell Street by a low stone wall with stone copings topped by plain iron railings painted black. The main entrance from Holland Road has a vehicular entrance with double gates, flanked by pedestrian gates. These are fixed to two pairs of ornamental stone piers and are of decorative wrought ironwork incorporating the letter M. There is a side entrance to the churchyard from Nell Street with an iron gate, this is of plain ironwork to match the railings. The southern and eastern boundaries have two metre high plain iron railings. Residential properties have rear yard walls of brick and stone.

Street Frontages

The Conservation Area is tightly developed with all the properties apart from the church, fronting the back of the pavement. The church is the only building with a garden and grounds.

Street Furniture

Most street lights within the area have concrete columns and modern metal lanterns. Along Blackburn Road the lights have tall steel columns. There are concrete bollards on the southern side of the footway to Birley Street near the junction with Blackburn Road and metal bollards on Holland Road to prevent vehicles parking on the pavement. There are traffic signs at either end of Birley Street.

Carriageways throughout the area are tarmacadamed. The footways to Birley Street are paved in stone flags, elsewhere they are tarmadamed.

Architectural Character

The buildings within the Conservation Area date from the Mid 19th Century. With the exception of numbers 492 and 504 Blackburn Road and the former infants school, they are Listed Grade II as being of Special Architectural of Historic Interest as follows:-

ST. PAULS CHURCH, HOLLAND STREET

The church was constructed in 1848 and the aisles were added in 1869 to the designs of J. Medland Taylor. It is built of coursed and squared stone with slate roofs and consists of a nave with clerestory and two aisles, a chancel with flanking chapel and vestry and a west tower and spire. The four stage tower has a west doorway, a bell chamber and a broach spire. The aisles have lancet windows and are divided by buttresses. The clerestory is divided into two bays by shallow buttresses and has round arched windows with a chevron *moulding forming the hoodmould and string* course. The interior of the building has a wide nave with a queen post roof, a large western gallery with pierced trefoiled panelling and late 19th Century stained glass windows.

The burial ground contains an interesting variety of stone monuments and headstones.

1 - 9 (ODD), BIRLEY STREET

This terrace of five houses dates from around 1850 and is constructed of coursed and squared rock faced sandstone with slate roofs and moulded stone gutters. The doorways have plain square cut stone architraves with rectangular oval lights. The window openings have wedge lintels and the original twelve pane sash openings have been replaced.

Figure 1.
1 - 9 Birley Street

2 - 18 (EVEN), BIRLEY STREET

This terrace of nine houses incorporates a shop and also dates from around 1850. It is built of coursed and squared stone with slate roofs and moulded stone gutters. The doorways have round arched moulded stone architraves with fanlights over the doors. The window openings have plain square cut stone architraves and the original twelve pane sash openings have been replaced.

The Non-Listed Buildings also make an important contribution to the character of the Conservation Area and merit retention and special care when repairs or alterations are being carried out.

492 - 504 BLACKBURN ROAD

The properties are similar in appearance to the adjacent terraced houses on Birley Street

Figure 2.
10 - 18 Birley Street

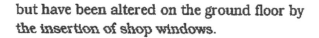

Figure 3.
492, 494 & 496, Blackburn Road

Figure 4.
Former St Pauls Infant School

but have been altered on the ground floor by the insertion of shop windows.

THE FORMER ST PAULS INFANT SCHOOL
This single storey building dates from around 1870 and is constructed of stone with pitched slate roofs. It has pointed arched windows with stone mullions and is now used as a cash and carry warehouse.

Negative Factors

A number of buildings in the Conservation Area have been altered in ways which detract from their traditional character. This includes painting brickwork and the installation of modern windows and doors. Inappropriate shop fronts and signs have been installed in properties fronting Blackburn Road.

SECTION TWO

Policy Guidelines

Statutory Controls

The Birley Street Conservation Area was designated in 1970. There are a range of Planning Controls to protect its character.

Conservation Area consent is needed from the Council to demolish or part demolish all but the smallest buildings. Part demolition includes the removal of features such as chimney stacks and bay windows. It also includes the demolition of elevations of a building.

The Council must be notified six weeks in advance of any proposals to cut down, top or lop trees in a Conservation Area.

A number of buildings within the Conservation Area are Listed Grade II. Listed Building consent is needed from the Council to demolish or extend a Listed Building or to alter it either outside or inside in any way which would change its character.

Bolton's Unitary Development Plan contains a number of policies relating to Conservation Areas and Listed Buildings. Numbers 492 - 504 Blackburn Road lie within the identified Astley Bridge District Centre and are subject to the District Centres shopping policies of the plan. All these policies are set out in the Appendix.

General guidance on policy for Conservation Areas and Listed Buildings is given in Planning Control Policy Notes 19 and 20. Guidance on shop front design and advertisements is given in Planning Control Policy Notes 4 and 6. These notes are available from the Planning Department.

Guidance leaflets on the care, maintenance and alteration of traditional buildings are also available free of charge.

Development Guidelines

DEMOLITION

- Consent will not usually be given to demolish buildings which make a positive contribution to the character of the Conservation Area.

ADVERTISEMENT CONTROL

- The Authority will apply high standards when considering applications for Advertisement Consent in the Conservation Area. Certain categories of advertisements are not permitted in Conservation Areas and discontinuance action will be taken against existing signs where they do not conform to the guidelines given in Planning Control Policy Note No 6. - "The Display of Signs and Advertisements".

NEW DEVELOPMENT

- New development must reflect the character of existing buildings with respect to siting, scale, proportions, materials and detailing. Applications for Outline Planning Permission will not be considered.

STREET SURFACING AND FURNITURE

- Any original stone flags, setts and kerbs should be retained and relaid where necessary.

- New paving on Birley Street should be in reclaimed or new stone. Concrete flags

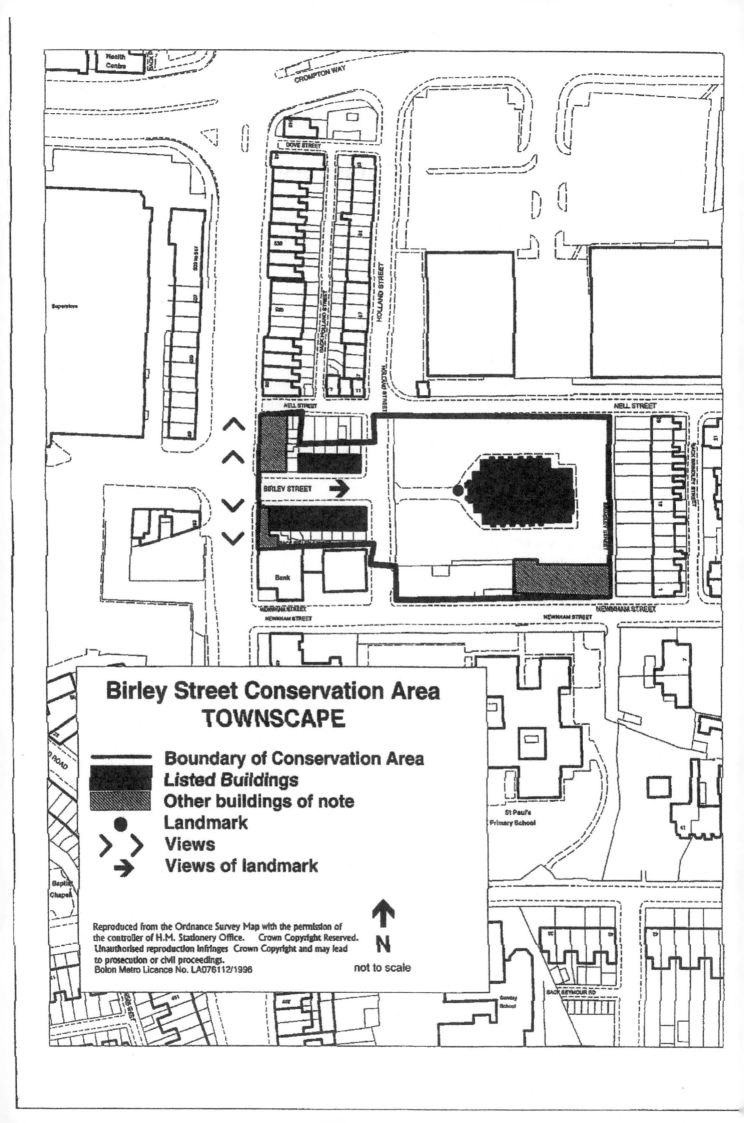

Birley Street Conservation Area
TOWNSCAPE

Boundary of Conservation Area
Listed Buildings
Other buildings of note
● Landmark
〉 〉 Views
➔ Views of landmark

Reproduced from the Ordnance Survey Map with the permission of
the controller of H.M. Stationery Office.   Crown Copyright Reserved.
Unauthorised reproduction infringes Crown Copyright and may lead
to prosecution or civil proceedings.
Bolon Metro Licence No. LA076112/1996

N

not to scale

replacing these should be in stone or blue clay.

- New rooflights may be acceptable but these should be flush fitting and should not be on prominent roof slopes.

RAINWATER GOODS

- Replacement rainwater goods should be in cast iron or moulded aluminium with a black coating.

BOUNDARY WALLS AND GATES

- Brick and stone boundary walls, iron railings and gates should be retained and any repairs carried out using the same materials and methods of workmanship.

SHOP FRONTS AND ADVERTISEMENTS

- The installation of traditional style painted timber shop fronts will be encouraged in appropriate buildings. This will include the use of stallrisers, pilasters and cornices to frame the shop window. Hand painted fascia signs and hanging signs will also be encouraged.

- Advertisement consent will not be given for internally illuminated box signs. The use of external lights and concealed lighting will be encouraged.

- Security shutters should preferably be fixed inside the shop windows and be of a perforated grille type to allow for a view of the window display. If external shutters are unavoidable, they should be incorporated into the overall design of the shop front with the shutter box concealed behind the fascia. The shutter system should be colour coated to match the colour of the shop front and the shutters should be perforated.

- Externally fixed shutter boxes which project from the facade of the shop, galvanised finishes and solid shutters are not in keeping with the character of the Conservation Area and are not acceptable.

MINOR FIXTURES

- Standard external fixtures including satellite dishes, meter boxes, burglar alarms, central heating flues and security cameras should be sited in unobtrusive positions wherever possible. They should be colour coated to match the background material i.e. walls or roofs.

WHEELIE BINS

- The layout of traditional properties can create difficulties for storing bins. Wherever possible they should be stored out of sight and not left on the street or footway.

incorporating an appropriate aggregate may be acceptable in other locations.

- Brick paving or black top should not be used as these materials are not in keeping with the character of the area.

- Any tarmacadam resurfacing to carriageways should incorporate an appropriate aggregate.

Building Materials

- Alterations should utilise traditional materials to match those used to construct the building. These include brick, stone and slate. Reclaimed local stone or new stone to match the existing should be used in preference to reconstituted stone.

- Strap or ribbon pointing should be avoided since this not only harms the appearance of the building but can damage the stone or brick by preventing the run off of water.

- External walls should not be painted, rendered or clad in modern materials.

- External cleaning should only be carried out to remove corrosive dirt. Cleaning should be carried out by a specialist firm under close supervision.

- Decorative features including plaques, mouldings and date stones should be retained.

WINDOWS AND DOORS

- Stone window cills, lintels, door surrounds and stone steps should be retained together with any original windows and doors.

- The integrity of the terraces depends on the retention of an uninterrupted flat facade relieved only by the subtle modelling of the surface, achieved by the recessing of doors and windows. The following are unacceptable:

  - porches
  - bow and bay windows
  - external shutters
  - changes in size or shape of window and door openings
  - dormer windows

- Any doorways or windows no longer in use should be retained and not blocked up.

- Owners should be encouraged to use the following styles when replacing windows and doors: Vertical sliding sash windows with glazing bars and six panes of glass to each of the opening lights, six panelled or vertically boarded doors.

- Windows and doors should be made of timber and should be painted.

- Staining is not a traditional finish for timber and should not be used. U.P.V.C. windows and doors are not acceptable as they are not in keeping with the character of traditional buildings.

- New windows and doors should be recessed to the original depth and should not be fitted flush with the face of the wall or project from it.

CHIMNEYS AND ROOFS

- Chimney stacks should be retained. If rebuilding is necessary this should be in the same materials used to construct the remainder of the building, this may be brick or stone with clay pots. Where central heating flues are installed, these should be contained within the original chimney pot or a traditional replacement.

- Roof repairs or replacements should be in natural slate to match the existing materials. Where ridge tiles need

SECTION THREE

Opportunities for Enhancement

This section highlights issues. It does not put forward detailed proposals for enhancement.

Listed Buildings Birley Street

The character and appearance of the two terraces of houses on Birley Street would be enhanced by the reinstatement of traditional timber sliding sash window and traditional timber doors.

Street Surfaces

The character of Birley Street would be enhanced by reinstating the original stone setts to the carriageway.

Street Lights

The appearance of the Conservation Area would be enhanced by the replacement of modern street lighting with traditional style columns and lanterns.

St Pauls Churchyard

The provision of seats in the churchyard would enable local people without gardens to enjoy this pleasant open space.

Shop Fronts, Advertisements, Shutters And Blinds

Detailed design advice on shop fronts, advertisements, shutters and blinds is needed to encourage higher standards throughout the Conservation Area.

Former St. Pauls Infant School

This building and its grounds would benefit from an improvement scheme including a more appropriate entrance and signing and the resurfacing of the car park.

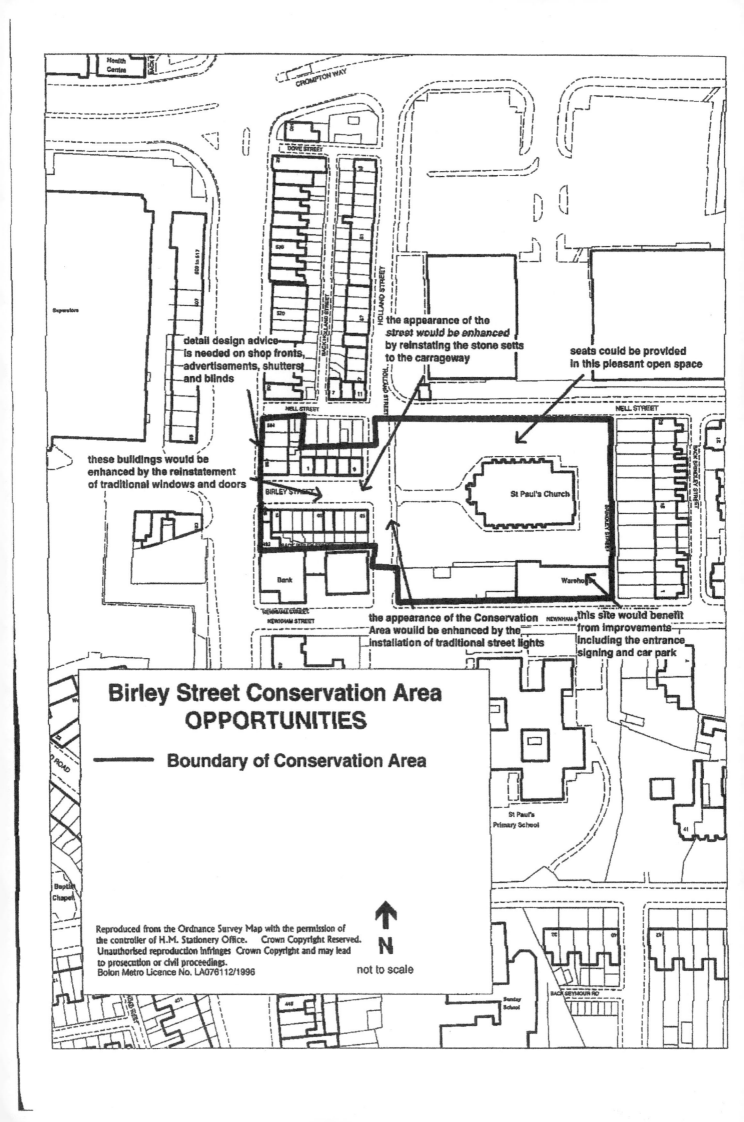

detail design advice is needed on shop fronts, advertisements, shutters and blinds

the appearance of the *street would be enhanced* by reinstating the stone setts to the carrageway

seats could be provided in this pleasant open space

these buildings would be enhanced by the reinstatement of traditional windows and doors

St Paul's Church

Bank

Warehouse

the appearance of the Conservation Area would be enhanced by the installation of traditional street lights

this site would benefit from improvements including the entrance signing and car park

St Paul's Primary School

Birley Street Conservation Area OPPORTUNITIES

—— Boundary of Conservation Area

N

not to scale

CROMPTON WAY
DOVE STREET
NELL STREET
BIRLEY STREET
NEWNHAM STREET
Sunday School
Baptist Chapel
Health Centre
Superstore
HOLLAND STREET
BACK HOLLAND STREET
BUNDLEY STREET
BACK BUNDLEY STREET
BACK SEYMOUR RD

APPENDIX

Bolton's Unitary Development Plan Policies

Conservation Areas

CE2. The Council will preserve or enhance the character of Conservation Areas.

Conservation Areas represent a significant element of Bolton's architectural and historical heritage. The Council will preserve and enhance these areas through the control of development and through positive schemes of enhancement. Development which is allowed should contribute positively to the quality of the environment. The Council is empowered to designate further Conservation Areas and will consider designating them as appropriate.

CE2/1 The council will preserve or enhance the character of Conservation Areas by;-

(a) **ensuring that all new development and alterations to existing buildings preserve or enhance the appearance of the Conservation Area;**

(b) **requiring the height, size, design, materials, roofscape or plot width of new development, including alterations or extensions to existing buildings, to respect the character of the Conservation Area;**

(c) **seeking to retain the materials, features, trees and open spaces which contribute to the character of the Conservation Area.**

This policy outlines some of the elements which the Council will take into account when considering applications in Conservation Areas.

CE2/2 The Council will not normally allow the demolition of buildings which contribute to the character of a Conservation Area. Where demolition is acceptable the Council will ensure that new

development enhances the appearance of the Conservation Area, and that building takes place as quickly as possible after demolition.

Consent from the Council is necessary for the demolition of buildings in Conservation Areas. If the building is important to the area's character, the demolition will be resisted. The Council will ensure that unsightly gaps are not left when demolition does take place by ensuring rapid development with good quality buildings.

CE2/3 The Council will not normally consider outline planning applications for development in Conservation Areas.

The Council will consider whether it has sufficient information to assess fully the environmental implications of a proposed development from an outline application.

Listed Buildings and Sites of Archaeological Interest

CE3. The Council will protect Listed Buildings and their setting, Ancient Monuments, and sites of archaeological interest from harmful development and operations.

Listed Buildings, Ancient Monuments and sites of Archaeological Interest are valuable as part of Bolton's heritage and there is a presumption for their retention and against any damage occurring to them. The Council will also try to ensure that necessary repairs are carried out to Listed Buildings whose condition is deteriorating. In appropriate circumstances the Council will encourage the Department of the Environment to list buildings which are considered to be of

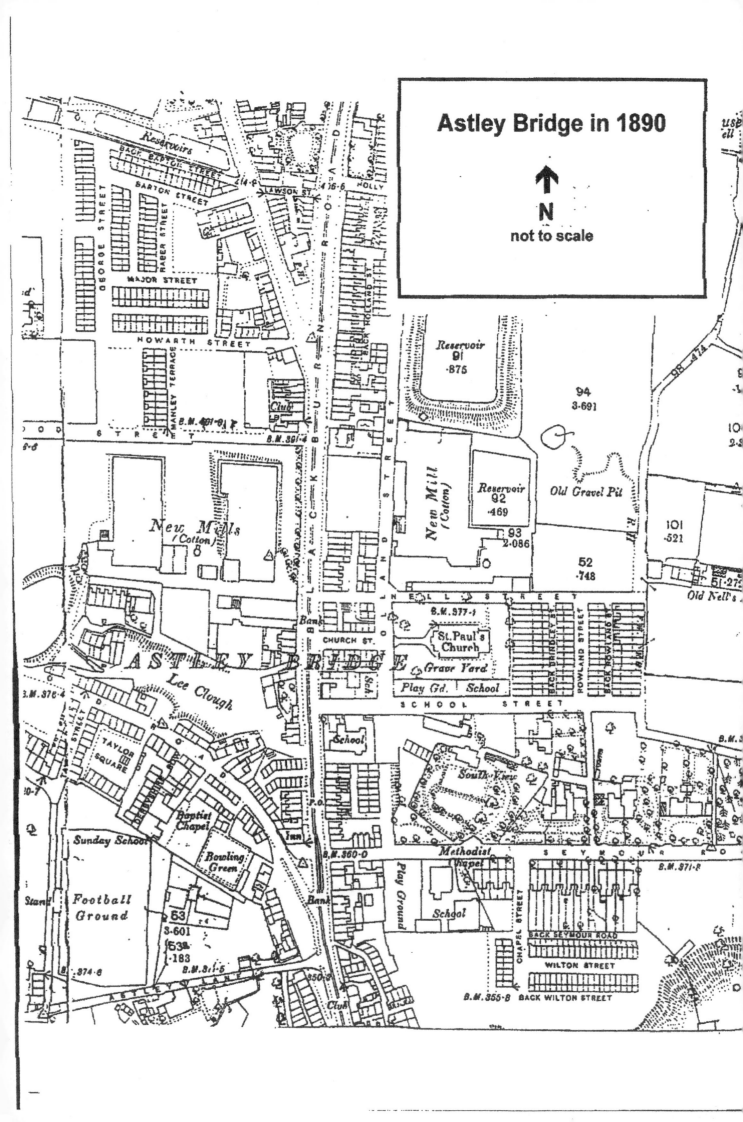

sufficient Architectural or Historical Interest. Where damage to archaeological sites is inevitable, action will be taken to try to ensure that the site is recorded fully.

CE3/1. Proposals for the alteration, extension or change of appearance of Listed Buildings should not detract from their character, appearance or setting. In considering applications for Listed Building Consent the Council will have regard to the following criteria:

(a) **proposals should retain the materials, features and details of the Listed Building;**

(b) **the height, size, design, setting and roofscape should respect the character of the Listed Building;**

(c) **proposals should not detract from the setting and open space which surround a Listed Building.**

This policy outlines the detailed criteria which will be taken into account in the determination of applications for Listed Building Consent. Apart from the basic design, it also highlights the importance of the setting and open space which surround Listed Buildings.

CE3/2. The Council will normally consider favourably proposals for appropriate alternative uses for Listed Buildings, provided that their character, appearance and setting are conserved. Some Listed Buildings are no longer required for their original uses. There is a danger that some buildings can lie empty and deteriorate, increasing the pressure to demolish them. The Council will try and avoid this by allowing alternative uses as long as they do not harm the character and appearance of the building and its setting and are in conformity with other policies of this Plan.

CE3/3 The Council will protect, enhance and preserve sites of archaeological interest and their setting and the importance of archaeological remains will be recognised in the consideration of planning applications.

Archaeological remains are irreplaceable and, in many cases, subject to damage and destruction during development. The Council will continue to support the maintenance and development of a comprehensive record of archaeological sites and monuments. The importance of archaeological sites and Ancient Monuments will be recognised in the consideration of planning applications. Where it is not considered essential to preserve remains, then arrangements will be entered into to record archaeological evidence.

District Centres

S5. The Council will normally permit proposals for shopping development, which are appropriate in scale and character, in or immediately adjoining the district centres.

There are four district centres in the Borough, namely Astley Bridge, Farnworth, Horwich and Westhoughton. They are smaller centres than Bolton, and offer local people convenient shopping for a wide range of goods. The Council wishes to sustain and support the role of the district centres as a principal focus for retailing, arts and cultural provision, leisure and entertainment, commercial services and community facilities. Support will be given to proposals involving the refurbishment of existing centres and the Council will, where possible promote schemes which improve the overall shopping environment.

In addition the Council believes that there are opportunities to extend facilities within district centres, especially for non-food retailing. It will therefore encourage proposals which will enhance the range of goods and services available within the centres. Proposals will normally have to be in or adjoining the identified shopping centre. the Council will interpret "adjoining" to mean immediately next to the shopping centre boundary. However, should a proposed site be separated from the shopping centre by a highway the Council will use its discretion as to whether the site is adjoining. A major factor in the analysis will be the class of the road, and whether it is perceived as a boundary which signifies a change in land-use. The Council will consider preparing more detailed strategies or Action Plans for each of the four centres over the plan period.

Astley Bridge Library and municipal offices
The offices date from 1896 during the short period - 4 years - when Astley Bridge was a separate
Urban District Council. In 1898 it was absorbed into Bolton Borough, who built the imposing
library in 1909.

BIRLEY STREET, LEADING TO ST. PAUL'S CHURCH C.E.

BUILT DURING THE MID 19th CENTURY, ALL THE HOUSES IN BIRLEY STREET ARE LISTED BUILDINGS. ST. PAUL'S WAS OPENED ON JUNE 22, 1848. IT COST £4,000 AND ORIGINALLY ACCOMMODATED 745 PEO... .E. IT WAS EXTENDED IN 1868 TO ACCOMMODATE 1,168 PEOPLE. ON THE NORTH WALL IS A MARBLE WAR MEMORIAL IN MEMORY OF THE ASTLEY BRIDGE PEOPLE LOST IN BOTH WORLD WARS [1914–1918, AND 1939–1945]. PRIOR TO ST. PAUL'S BEING BUILT, SERVICES WERE HELD IN A NEARBY BUILDING KNOWN AS ASH GROVE CHAPEL. *[SEE THE BRIEF HISTORY OF ASTLEY BRIDGE SECTION.]*

CHURCH OF ALL SOULS C.E. (NOT IN AB)
THIS CHURCH, ON ASTLEY STREET, WAS BUILT IN 1880.

SHARPLES HALL

BUILT AROUND 1865 AND ORIGINALLY CALLED OLLERTON HALL, THE NAME WAS CHANGED BY SIR JOHN HOLDEN WHEN HE BOUGHT IT FROM PERCY ASHWORTH. IT HAS FOR A LONG TIME CONTAINED FLATS AND WAS RECENTLY RENOVATED AND EXTENDED.

SHARPLES HALL FARMHOUSE

THIS FARMHOUSE, IN SHARPLES HALL FOLD, OFF BLACKBURN ROAD, WAS BUILT IN 1843. IT IS THOUGHT THAT THERE WAS AN EVEN OLDER SHARPLES HALL IN THE AREA, BUT IT IS NOT KNOWN EXACTLY WHERE.

Nos. 87 – 105 [ODD] WAVERLEY ROAD

THESE HOUSES WERE BUILT DURING THE LATE 18th CENTURY

THORNLEIGH SALESIAN COLLEGE R.C.

BUILT BETWEEN 1868 AND 1870, AS A PRIVATE HOUSE, IT WAS TAKEN OVER AS A COLLEGE IN 1925, AND HAS BEEN EXTENDED A NUMBER OF TIMES, MOST RECENTLY IN 1989. THIS PICTURE WAS TAKEN AT THE BEGINNING OF THE PRESENT CENTURY.

BOSCO HOUSE

BOSCO HOUSE, FORMERLY *THE LEES VILLA*, WAS BUILT IN THE LATE 18th CENTURY. IT WAS BOUGHT AS AN ADDITION TO THE COLLEGE AROUND 1939, AND IS NOW THE LIVING QUARTERS OF THORNLEIGH'S COLLEGE FATHERS.

HARRICROFT FARMHOUSE

THE FARMHOUSE AND BUILDINGS TO THE NORTH WERE BUILT BEFORE 1765. THE NEARBY BARN WAS BUILT IN 1832 AND IS INSCRIBED WITH THE INITIALS OF RICHARD AINSWORTH [1762–1833], A RELATIVE OF PETER AINSWORTH [1713–1787], WHO STARTED THE BLEACHWORKS AT MOSS BANK IN THE EARLY 1740'S.

No. 11A ECKERSLEY ROAD

THIS HOUSE WAS BUILT AROUND THE MID 19th CENTURY. IT ADJOINS No. 367 BLACKBURN ROAD, ALSO A LISTED BUILDING.

Nos. 25 – 31 [Odd], PEMBERTON STREET.

THESE HOUSES WERE BUILT AROUND THE EARLY 19th CENTURY.

No. 31 RAMSEY STREET

THIS HOUSE WAS BUILT DURING THE EARLY 19th CENTURY.

EDEN'S ORPHANAGE

EDEN'S ORPHANAGE, THORNS ROAD, WAS A BUILDING IN FREE GOTHIC STYLE. IT WAS OPENED IN 1879 AS A BEQUEST BY JAMES EDEN, OF THE FIRM EDEN & THWAITES, WHO OWNED THE WATERS MEETING BLEACH WORKS. HE DIED IN 1874, BEQUEATHING £10,000 FOR THE COST OF THE BUILDING, PLUS AN ENDOWMENT FUND OF AROUND £40,000. THE INSTITUTION, BY THE TERMS OF THE WILL, WAS FOR THE CARE, SUPPORT AND UP BRINGING OF DESTITUTE ORPHANS, WHOSE PARENTS AT THE TIME OF DEATH, LIVED IN THE AREA OF THE BOLTON POOR LAW UNION. THE SITE, OF JUST OVER FOUR ACRES, USED TO CONTAIN A FARM CALLED TAYLOR'S TENEMENT. IN 1948, A THIRD OF THE BUILDING WAS TAKEN OVER AND CONVERTED INTO A DAY NURSERY BY THE FIRM OF GREENHALGH & SHAW LTD. IN 1951 THE BUILDING WAS TAKEN OVER BY THE ISIS PRIVATE SCHOOL. THIS SCHOOL ORIGINALLY HAD PREMISES IN MAWDSLEY STREET WHICH HAD OPENED IN 1948. IT WAS FORCED TO CLOSE IN 1966 DUE TO INCREASED RUNNING COSTS. THE BUILDING WAS LATER DEMOLISHED AND THE SITE NOW CONTAINS FLATS. THE ORIGINAL GATEHOUSE IS NOW A PRIVATE RESIDENCE.

ST. PAUL'S INFANT SCHOOL

ST. PAUL'S INFANT SCHOOL BLACKBURN ROAD, WAS OPENED IN 1871. IT ORIGINALLY CONTAINED A LECTURE HALL. THE COST OF THE BUILDING AND FURNITURE WAS £1,404, WHICH WAS RAISED BY A COMBINATION OF PRIVATE SUBSCRIPTION AND GRANTS FROM THE DIOCESAN BOARD AND THE EDUCATION & NATIONAL SOCIETY. THE GIRLS SCHOOL, JUST AROUND THE CORNER IN NEWNHAM STREET, WAS BUILT IN 1881 AT A COST OF £3,118, THE MAJORITY OF WHICH WAS RAISED BY PRIVATE SUBSCRIPTION.

SHARPLES VALE, EARLY THIS CENTURY

SHARPLES VALE ONCE CONTAINED A MILL AND BLEACH WORKS WHICH WERE BOTH DEMOLISHED EARLY THIS CENTURY. THE MILL OPENED AROUND 1880 AND CHANGED HANDS A NUMBER OF TIMES. IT WAS OWNED BY JAMES BRIMELOW, GREENHALGH & SHAW AND JOHN SCHOFIELD. THE BLEACH WORKS OPENED BETWEEN 1821 AND 1822 AND ALSO CHANGED HANDS A NUMBER OF TIMES. IT WAS OWNED BY NIGHTINGALE AND SOUTHWORTH, EDEN & THWAITES, JAMES AND LEWIS MURTON, AND GEORGE MURTON & Co. THE VALE IS NOW OCCUPIED BY A BUILDERS' YARD, A SMALL FOUNDRY AND SHEET METAL WORKS, A TOFFEE MANUFACTURER, AND PRIVATE HOUSES. THERE WAS PREVIOUSLY ANOTHER SHARPLES VALE, ON THE OPPOSITE SIDE OF BLACKBURN ROAD, NEAR HALL I' TH' WOOD. THIS CAN BE SEEN ON THE 1845 MAP OF THE AREA.

SHARPLES VALE, 1992

ASTLEY BRIDGE CEMETERY CHAPEL

THIS CHAPEL, BUILT IN GEOMETRIC GOTHIC STYLE, WAS OPENED IN 1884 FOR MIXED DENOMINATIONS. IT IS 40 FEET BY 21 FEET AND ACCOMMODATES 80 PEOPLE. THE TOTAL COST OF BUILDING AND LAND WAS £10,000. THE CEMETERY ADJOINED THE EDEN ORPHANAGE (NOW THE SITE OF FLATS) AND WAS PURCHASED FROM THE EDEN TRUSTEES. THE ARCHITECTURE WAS BY J. SIMPSON AND THE CORNER STONE WAS LAID BY COLONEL HESKETH, J.P. AND CHAIRMAN OF THE ASTLEY BRIDGE LOCAL BOARD.

SEYMOUR ROAD METHODIST CHURCH

THIS CHURCH WAS OFFICIALLY OPENED IN 1868. IN 1969 IT WAS CONVERTED TO A THEATRE CHURCH. (SEE THE BLACKBURN ROAD SECTION.)

PHOTOGRAPHS OF ASTLEY BRIDGE

WATERS MEETING WORKS

THESE WORKS, SEEN HERE FROM CROMPTON WAY, WERE ORIGINALLY CALLED WATERS MEETING BLEACH WORKS. THEY WERE THOUGHT TO HAVE BEEN ORIGINALLY ESTABLISHED IN 1770, BUT THE EARLIEST DEEDS ARE DATED 1806. IN 1830 THEY WERE TAKEN OVER BY EDEN & THWAITES. IN 1925 THEY WERE JOINED BY HAY & SMITH Ltd. THE WORKS CLOSED IN 1962 BUT LATER REOPENED FOR MULTIPLE INDUSTRIAL USES. THEY ARE STILL IN USE AT THE TIME OF PUBLICATION. ON THE RIGHT IS HALL HOUSE FARM WHICH WAS ONCE OWNED BY EDEN & THWAITES.

WATERMILLOCK

WATERMILLOCK WAS BUILT IN 1881 BY THOMAS THWAITES, WHO NAMED IT AFTER HIS ORIGINAL RESIDENCE IN THE LAKE DISTRICT. IN 1824 HE WAS BOLTON BOROUGH REEVE, A POSITION EQUIVALENT TO THAT OF A CHIEF MAGISTRATE. HE DID NOT LIVE TO SEE THE COMPLETION OF THE HOUSE WHICH WAS OCCUPIED BY HIS SON HERBERT. ACROSS CROMPTON WAY, WHICH WAS OPENED IN 1928, IS THE ORIGINAL GATE HOUSE, NOW A PRIVATE RESIDENCE. THOMAS THWAITE OWNED THE NEARBY WATERS MEETING BLEACH WORKS. DURING THE FIRST WORLD WAR [1914–18], WATERMILLOCK WAS USED AS A RED CROSS HOSPITAL FOR WOUNDED SOLDIERS. IT WAS LATER A MANCHESTER DIOCESAN RETREAT FOR CLERGY OF THE CHURCH OF ENGLAND. DURING THE SPANISH CIVIL WAR [1936–39] THE HOUSE WAS USED TO ACCOMMODATE REFUGEES. BETWEEN THE 1950'S AND 1988, IT WAS USED AS A COUNCIL RESIDENTIAL RETIREMENT HOME. AT THE MOMENT IT IS FOR SALE.

BARLOW PARK

BARLOW PARK, WHICH OPENED IN 1927, WAS DONATED TO THE PEOPLE OF BOLTON BY JOHN ROBERT BARLOW, [THE CHAIRMAN OF DOBSON AND BARLOW'S WORKS] AND PATRICK BASIL BARLOW.

WEST GLEN (W.G) ASTLEY BRIDGE BEAUTY SPOT ABOUT 1900

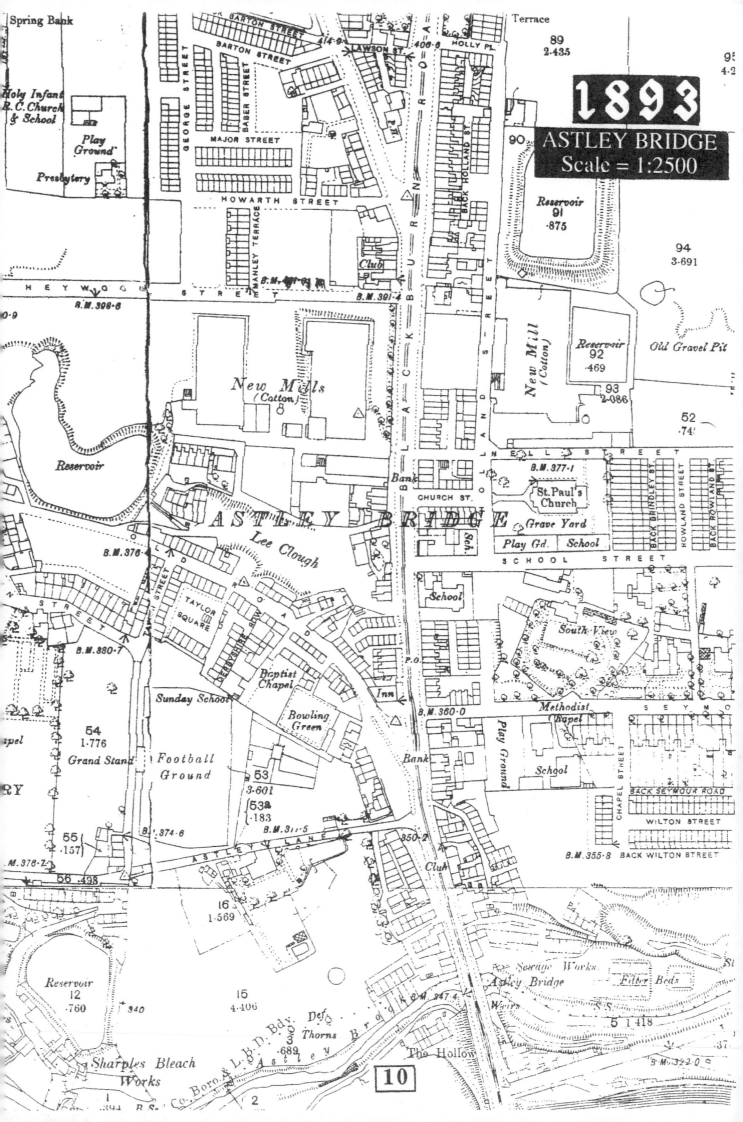